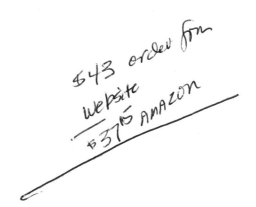

$43 order from website
$37⁵ Amazon

PROLI FOOTWEAR, INC.

An Audit and Fraud Simulation
for Team-Based Student Participation

SECOND EDITION

See Folder; my documents/textbooks /poli for Student Excel worksheet files

Patricia M. Poli, CPA, Ph.D.
Charles F. Dolan School of Business
Fairfield University

Richard J. Proctor, MBA, CPA, CVA, CGFM
Ancell School of Business
Western Connecticut State University

D1248521

DEDICATION

The second edition of this simulation is dedicated to
Elfriede Proctor, Richard Proctor's late wife,
Vijay Nair, Pat Poli's husband,
Maureen Turnier,
Charlotte, Logan, Oliver, Tyler,
Frankie, Maya, Joshua, Austin, Alex,
and the rest of our families.

.

ACKNOWLEDGEMENT

We wish to express our deep gratitude to
the many auditing students who used the first edition.
Their diligent efforts and feedback helped make
the first edition a success and
assisted us in improving the second edition.

Note to Student: Excel spreadsheet templates are available
FREE of charge at ProliFootwear.com

ABOUT THE AUTHORS

A.K.A. RP

Richard J. Proctor, MBA, CPA, CVA, CGFM

Richard J. Proctor is Professor of Accounting at the Ancell School of Business at Western Connecticut State University. His research and teaching interests include valuation of closely held business interests, valuation of economic damages, auditing, fraud examination, financial accounting, and federal taxation.

Professor Proctor received his B.S. in accounting and M.B.A. in finance from Columbia University and holds various designations including Certified Public Accountant, and Certified Valuation Analyst. He has over 25 years experience as a consulting forensic accountant.

A.K.A. Patricia Fair

Patricia M. Poli, CPA, Ph.D.

Patricia M. Poli is Associate Professor of Accounting at the Dolan School of Business at Fairfield University where she teaches financial accounting and auditing. Her research interests are the strategic financial considerations of multinational firms, the effects of the accounting choices they make, and audit education. Dr. Poli is active in several professional organizations, including the Connecticut Society of CPAs and the American Accounting Association.

Dr. Poli received her B.S. in accounting from the University of Connecticut and her Ph.D. in accounting from New York University. She is active as a consulting forensic accountant.

TABLE OF CONTENTS

INTRODUCTION

OVERVIEW

Proli Footwear is an audit and fraud simulation designed to involve you in a simulated audit engagement that combines audit theory and practice as well as integrating the application of generally accepted accounting principles.

This simulation is divided into 9 sections and 12 work modules, which will be completed over the course of the semester. Your audit team will hand in assignments for grading.

The audit programs included in the simulation contain selected procedures that apply to the particular assignment. Each assignment has an audit budget and you will compare your team's actual hours with these budgets. In addition to audit procedures, you will also learn about some of the other administrative functions that the in-charge and the manager on the job will perform, such as determining which audit procedures to perform during interim periods and which to perform after year-end. Also, you will deal with certain elements of fraud that will arise during the engagement.

PROLI FOOTWEAR, INC.

Proli ("Proli") Footwear, Inc. was incorporated in Connecticut in 1941 and is primarily a family-owned business. The Company's headquarters are located in Proli, Connecticut, a mythical town on the north end of the mythical Candleweed Lake. Proli originally began in business making leather combat boots and work shoes for use by the U.S. Army during WWII. In the late 1940s, its business transitioned from being primarily a military footwear supplier to the manufacture of various durable work boots for use by workers in industry. Today, it designs, develops, engineers, manufactures, markets, and distributes branded premium quality protective footwear for the sporting, outdoor, and occupational markets. All manufacturing is done in the United States in the Company's three facilities located in Proli, CT, Waterbury, CT, and Walton, FL. Proli was and remains a very important employer in Western Connecticut.

The Company has a number of Company officers and key personnel:

- Samuel Sole, Jr. – Chairman of the Board and founder
- Josephine Chopines – President and CEO
- Goodwin Buye – Vice President-Purchasing
- Harold F. Heele – Vice President-Finance and Administration and CFO
- Samuel Sole, III – Vice President-Product Development
- Verna F. Vamp – Vice President-Information Technology, a newcomer to the Company
- Brian Baddude – Controller (he is sensitive about the pronunciation of his name: it is pronounced Bahdood)

Proli Footwear is planning to go public within the next five years and has hired the independent accounting firm, West & Fair, CPAs, LLC, to assist in preparing Proli and its employees for this undertaking.

THE AUDITORS: WEST & FAIR, CPAs, LLC

West & Fair was founded in 1985 when sole practitioner Richard West merged with sole practitioner Patricia Fair and founded the firm of West & Fair, CPAs, LLC. The firm has grown from two partners and three staff employees to its current size of 7 partners and 52 staff employees. RP is a senior staff person assigned to the Proli audit. The firm is based at 7555 Working Street in Stamford, Connecticut. The firm enjoys a diverse client base primarily located in New York, New Jersey, Connecticut, and the other New England States.

This is the first year that West & Fair will audit Proli Footwear. Proli is anticipating going public within five years and has hired West & Fair to assist in this process. Proli expects West & Fair to make recommendations for improvements to Proli's operations and controls in addition to conducting an audit of its financial statements. West & Fair was hired by Proli in November 2013 to perform the 2014 audit. West & Fair observed the 2013 physical inventory count and performed sales and purchase cut-off tests to verify 2014 opening balances.

THE AUDIT TEAM

The following comprises the Proli Footwear, Inc. audit team.

Name	Position
Patricia Fair	Engagement Partner
Richard West	Review Partner
RP	In-Charge Senior Auditor
Student Team Members	Audit Staff

ORGANIZING AND STARTING THE AUDIT

The class will be divided into audit teams of 3-5 students. The sequence of the assignments generally follows a cycle approach with a balance sheet format for some sections. However, these assignments will not necessarily follow the sequence of the textbook you are using. Therefore, you may be performing audit procedures before reading about them in the textbook. The steps in the audit program will assist you in the assignment. You may want to read the appropriate chapter in the textbook prior to doing the assignment and thereby use the text as a reference manual. You will also need to use an intermediate accounting textbook as you work on this simulation.

The first assignment concentrates on permanent file material and company history in order to give you an overview of Proli Footwear operations and procedures. The second assignment focuses on audit planning and internal control. Assignments 3 through 8 relate to the application of audit procedures to specific areas of the balance sheet and income statement. Assignment 9 completes the audit with the drafting of the report and the final analytic review.

AUDIT DOCUMENTATION FORMAT AND TECHNIQUE

The auditor, through the use of audit documentation, records the collection of audit evidence. These audit documents have two primary functions:

1. To provide a record that the audit was conducted in accordance with generally accepted auditing standards (GAAS) and supports the auditor's opinion and

2. To assist the auditors in planning and supervising the audit.

There are normally two categories of audit documentation: permanent and current. The permanent audit documentation contains information that is of continuing relevance to auditors when conducting recurring engagements. Current audit documentation contains information relevant only to the particular year being audited.

Audit documentation should include information that shows that:

1. The audit was adequately planned and supervised as required by the first standard of fieldwork;

2. The auditor has obtained an understanding of the internal control system that will enable the auditor to plan and determine the nature, timing, and extent of the audit procedures to be performed; and

3. The evidence obtained was sufficient, competent, and timely. In addition this evidence must support the audit report issued.

More specifically, the audit documentation must be readable and clearly establish the work performed. The audit documentation must show the scope of the work done, the sources of the information contained on them and the auditor's conclusion about the work performed.

The format of the audit documentation must include the following components:

1. Headings: include the client name, date of financial statements being audited, and purpose (title) of the schedule.

2. Indices: include the assignment of a code to each group of audit documents to permit control over the audit documentation during the audit and to provide a consistent basis for arranging the documentation. West & Fair uses the following codes:

I	=	Administrative File
II	=	Planning File
PF	=	Permanent File
A	=	Cash
B	=	Accounts Receivable
C	=	Inventory
D	=	Long-Lived Assets
E	=	Liabilities
F	=	Equity and Miscellaneous Accruals

3. Tickmarks are symbols on the audit documentation that explain the work done by the auditors. They should be simple enough so that the reviewer can easily determine the procedures performed.

4. Sign-offs consist of initials to indicate who prepared and who reviewed the working papers and the date that the work was performed.

5. Cross-references assist the reviewer in finding related information on different audit documents.

6. Notation to indicate that the client prepared the schedule: West & Fair uses the notation, PBC, prepared by client.

AUDIT DOCUMENTATION HELPFUL HINTS

1. Any page that you use or perform analysis on must have your sign-off and date of completion. Some schedules have been *completed* by RP (they are the schedules that have his sign-off denoted by his initials as follows RP). There is **no** need for you to redo or check his work. You must, however, put in the date on which you think that RP did the work.

2. Any work performed must be shown through the use of tickmarks. This allows the reviewer to know exactly what work you performed.

3. You must include a tickmark legend on any schedule where you use tickmarks. A tickmark legend is a list of all tickmarks used on the schedule along with a concise but specific explanation of the work performed. Do not assume that the reviewer will know what the tickmark means.

4. Referencing information between schedules is very important. The lead schedule numbers must be referenced to the TB. Amounts on a specific audit document must be referenced to the lead schedule. Any supporting schedules must be referenced. (e.g. if the customer confirmation says that payment has been made, reference the payment to the cash receipts journal). However, at the same time, you must avoid excessive cross-referencing.

5. Journal entries should be numbered sequentially within each section (e.g. journal entries in Assignment 3 should be numbered 3-1, 3-2, etc.)

6. Record each complete adjusting journal entry (i.e. DR = CR) on the following schedules:

   - Specific audit document where the adjustment arises
   - AJE summary for the assignment
   - Lead schedule
   - Working Trial Balance

7. Be sure to include management letter comments with each assignment. Management comments should identify the underlying issue but it must focus on recommendations to alleviate that problem. Generally, the comments will concentrate on improving internal control and operating policies. The benefit to the client section *must* give the client some compelling reason to institute the change. The client is not as concerned about GAAP and GAAS as they are about ways to promote efficiency, ways to save money, etc. Be specific in your comments.

TICKMARK CONVENTIONS

Most firms use standardized tickmarks that are understood by all members of the firm. The systematic use of tickmarks leaves a trail of the auditor's work, which enables a supervisor to review staff performance on each aspect of the audit. West & Fair has adopted the following common tickmarks for use in each of its audits:

F	=	Footed column
CF	=	Crossfooted row
TB	=	Amount agrees to Trial Balance
E	=	Examined (supporting document name)
T	=	Traced the amount from (document name) to a (journal name) or (schedule reference)
V	=	Vouched payment from (accounting record) to (document name)
R	=	Verified calculations by recomputation
C	=	Confirmation sent to (customer, vendor, etc.)

Other tickmarks can be created and added to the list as needed; nonstandard tickmarks and their explanation must be included on the specific worksheet.

REPORT CARD ON GROUP MEMBERS

Periodically you may be asked to assign a grade to your teammates and yourself for performance. As in any evaluation, you must be honest and remember that this information is confidential. Your instructor will give you the appropriate evaluation form as well as the grading guidelines.

STUDENT ANALYSIS AND PRESENTATION OPTIONS

At your instructor's discretion, your presentations may consist of one or two of the following: a meeting with the client or the audit manager (role-played by the instructor) and the actual presentation of the solution to the specific assignment.

The meeting with the client or the audit manager provides your team with the opportunity to obtain additional information and to clarify information. This meeting is one of the professional activities that is common in the audit and should be treated as the professional meeting that it represents. You should be able to obtain the information needed in less than 30 minutes.

Your audit team's findings should be given in a 15 to 30 minute presentation using appropriate audio and visual aids. The audit team should be prepared to answer any questions from the class and the instructor regarding the items discussed. The team should discuss the following:

1. Adjusting entries: the actual entries and a discussion explaining the need for the entries;

2. Any additional internal control issues encountered during the audit;

3. Comments to be included in the management letter: the team should specifically address the benefit(s) to be obtained by the client's acceptance of the recommendations; and

4. Your audit conclusions regarding the work performed.

SUBMITTING YOUR GROUP ASSIGNMENTS

Your instructor will advise you whether to hand in the electronic spreadsheets or the manual worksheets.

1. Each group assignment must have a typed cover sheet which contains the following information: Assignment Name, Due Date, Group Member Names;

2. Audit documentation for each assignment being submitted should be organized in the following sequence:
   - Audit program with dates, initials and audit documentation references;
   - Completed Lead Schedule with workpaper references, tickmarks indicating work done and appropriate sign-offs;
   - Specific audit work paper schedules in sequence with workpaper references, as appropriate, tickmarks indicating work done and appropriate sign-offs;
   - Adjusting Journal Entry summary containing the proposed AJEs;
   - Red Flag Events;
   - Management Letter Comments containing recommended improvements to internal control and other operating issues;
   - Updated Time Control Worksheet; and
   - Updated Working Trial Balance (WTB).

AUDIT BUDGET

The engagement's in-charge accountant has prepared the budget for each assignment. Since this is the first audit for the client, this budget is based on the in-charge accountant's experiences with similar engagements. The budget represents the time to be spent by you and your team members (working as a group) to complete all audit schedules and to discuss, research, and resolve any accounting or audit issues. You should have an audit textbook and an intermediate accounting textbook available during your group meetings.

- Assignment 1: Creating the Permanent File .... 3 hours
- Assignment 2: Planning the Audit.. 5 hours
- Assignment 3: Cash.. 6 hours
- Assignment 4: Accounts Receivable and Sales............................. 6 hours
- Assignment 5: Inventory and Accounts Payable............................ 7 hours
- Assignment 6A: Property, Plant, and Equipment .... 5 hours
- Assignment 6B: Intangible Assets .... 4 hours
- Assignment 7A: Current Liabilities .... 4 hours
- Assignment 7B: Lease Liabilities .... 3 hours
- Assignment 7C: Mortgage Liabilities... 3 hours
- Assignment 8: Finishing the Audit .... 4 hours
- Assignment 9: Drafting the Report .... 2 hours

TIMELINE FOR THE AUDIT

The engagement partner has assigned your team to work on the Proli audit during the following time periods:

- January 2, 2014
- January 12 - 16, 2014
- August 10 - 21, 2014
- January 2, 2015
- January 4 - 8, 2015
- January 25 – February 26, 2015

GRADING GUIDELINES

Assignment 1 which has only short-answer questions, will be graded as follows:

1. Correct answers to short-answer questions 90
2. All steps in the audit program have been initialed and dated 10

Assignments 2-9 require a more detailed grading model and your instructor will grade the group assignments using the following general guidelines:

1. Audit documentation is properly organized and referenced and reflects a quality effort..10
2. All steps in the audit program have been initialed and dated 10
3. The audit team has performed the following work procedures: 20
   - Compared the balance per trial balance to the balances per lead schedule and supporting schedules;
   - Footed and crossfooted all data columns;
   - Checked all PBC schedules for clerical accuracy;
   - Reconciled the balance per trial balance to the final audited balance on all schedules.
4. Tickmarks are appropriately placed and described..20
5. Recommendations for improvements to the internal control system and operations have been made. Benefit to client has been clearly stated.................10
6. Adjusting Journal Entries (AJEs) 30
   - AJEs have been correctly determined and contain complete explanations;
   - AJEs must be displayed on the appropriate audit document, lead schedule,
   - AJE control, and WTB;
   - AJEs are sequentially numbered.

CLIENT PREPARED DRAFT FINANCIAL STATEMENTS (1/7)

Proli Footwear, Inc.
Balance Sheet
December 31, 2014

	(000)
Current Assets	
Cash and cash equivalents	319
Trade accounts receivable, less allowances of $1.1 million	25,466
Inventories (Note 2)	43,668
Prepaid expenses	4,718
Total current assets	74,171
Property, Plant and Equipment	
Land and buildings	8,834
Machinery and equipment	32,328
	41,162
Less accumulated depreciation	25,781
	15,381
Other Assets	
Intangibles, net of amortization of $5.2 million	14,567
Other assets	3,284
	17,851
Total Assets	107,403
Liabilities and Shareholders' Equity	
Current Liabilities	
Current maturities of long-term obligations (Note 4)	441
Notes payable, bank (Note 4)	12,800
Accounts payable	3,816
Accrued expenses (Note 6)	7,919
Total current liabilities	24,976
Long-Term Debt Obligations (Note 4)	4,666
Long-Term Lease Obligations (Note 5)	1,296
Deferred Compensation and Benefits (Note 7)	3,357
Commitments and Contingencies	
Total Liabilities	34,295
Stockholders' Equity	
Common stock, par value $1.00 per share; authorized 1,000,000 shares; issued and outstanding, 50,000 shares	50
Additional paid-in capital	22,500
Retained earnings	50,558
Total stockholders' equity	73,108
Total Liabilities and Stockholders' Equity	107,403

See Notes to Financial Statements.

CLIENT PREPARED DRAFT FINANCIAL STATEMENTS (2/7)

Proli Footwear, Inc.
Income Statement
Year Ended December 31, 2014

	(000)
Net sales	146,745
Cost of goods sold	108,712
Gross profit	38,033
Selling and administrative expenses	32,876
Operating income	5,157
Non-operating income (expense)	(1,465)
Income before income taxes	3,692
Income tax expense (Note 3)	1,600
Net income	2,092

See Notes to Financial Statements.

x

CLIENT PREPARED DRAFT FINANCIAL STATEMENTS (3/7)

Proli Footwear, Inc.
Statement of Cash Flows
Year Ended December 31, 2014

We don't know how to prepare this statement. We will let you assist us.

See Notes to Financial Statements.

CLIENT PREPARED DRAFT FINANCIAL STATEMENTS (4/7)

Proli Footwear, Inc.
Statement of Shareholders' Equity
Year Ended December 31, 2014

	Common Stock	Additional Paid-In Capital	Retained Earnings	Total Shareholders' Equity
Balances, December 31, 2013	50	22,500	49,966	72,516
Net income			2,092	2,092
Common stock dividends ($40.00 per share)			(1,500)	(1,500)
Balances, December 31, 2014	50	22,500	50,558	73,108

See Notes to Financial Statements.

NOTES TO FINANCIAL STATEMENTS

Note 1. Nature of Business and Significant Accounting Policies

Nature of business:

The Company designs, manufactures and markets premium quality protective footwear for sale principally throughout the United States.

Significant accounting policies:

Use of estimates in the preparation of financial statements: The preparation of financial statements in conformity with generally accepted accounting principles requires management to make estimates and assumptions that affect the reported amounts of assets and liabilities and disclosure of contingent assets and liabilities at the date of the financial statements and the amounts of revenues and expenses during the reporting period. Actual results could differ from those estimates.

Fair value of financial instruments:

The following methods and assumptions were used to estimate the fair value of each class of financial instruments: The carrying amount of cash and cash equivalents approximates fair   value because of the short maturity of those investments. The carrying amount of long-term debt approximates fair value based on the interest rates, maturities and collateral requirements currently available for similar financial instruments.

Concentrations of credit risk:

The Company grants credit to its customers, who are primarily domestic retail stores, direct mail catalog merchants and wholesalers, based on an evaluation of the customer's financial condition. Exposure to losses on receivables is principally dependent on each customer's financial condition. The Company monitors its exposure for credit losses and maintains an allowance for anticipated losses.

Cash and cash equivalents:

The Company considers all highly liquid debt instruments (including short-term investment grade securities and money market instruments) purchased with maturities of three months or less to be cash equivalents. The Company maintains its cash in bank deposit accounts which, at times, exceed federally insured limits. The Company has not experienced any losses in such accounts.

Property and equipment:

Property and equipment are carried at cost and are being depreciated using straight-line and accelerated methods over their estimated useful lives as follows: buildings, 5 to 35 years; and machinery and equipment, 10 to 15 years.

Impairment of long-lived assets:

The Company reviews its long-lived assets and intangibles periodically to determine potential impairment by comparing the carrying value of these assets with expected future net cash flows provided by operating activities of the business. Should the sum of the expected future net cash flows be less than the carrying value, the Company would determine whether an impairment loss should be recognized. An impairment loss would be measured by comparing the amount by which the carrying value exceeds the fair value of the long-lived assets and intangibles based on appraised market value.

Income taxes:

Deferred taxes are provided on a liability method whereby deferred tax assets and liabilities are recognized for temporary differences. Temporary differences are the differences between the reported amounts of assets and liabilities and their tax bases. Deferred tax assets are reduced by a valuation allowance when, in the opinion of management, it is more likely than not that some portion or all of the deferred tax assets will not be realized. Deferred tax assets and liabilities are adjusted for the effects of changes in tax laws and rates on the date of enactment.

Earnings per share:

The Financial Accounting Standards Board ("FASB") has issued Statement of Financial Accounting Standards ("SFAS") No. 128, Earnings per Share, which supersedes APB Opinion No. 15. Statement No. 128 requires the presentation of earnings per share by all entities that have common stock or potential common stock (such as options and convertible securities) outstanding that trade in a public market. Those entities that have only common stock   outstanding are required to present basic earnings per share amounts.

Revenue recognition and product warranty:

Revenue is recognized at the time products are shipped to customers. Revenue is recorded net of freight, estimated discounts and returns. The Company warrants its products against defects in design, materials and workmanship generally for one year.

Note 2. Inventories

A summary of inventories is as follows:

	(In Thousands)
Finished goods	37,118
Work in process	-0-
Raw materials	6 ,550
Total inventories	43,668

Note 3. Income Tax Matters

Net deferred tax assets and liabilities consist of the following components:

(In Thousands)

Deferred tax assets:
Deferred tax liabilities:

Income tax expense consists of the following:

(In Thousands)

Current:
Federal
State
Deferred

The differences between statutory federal tax rates and the effective tax rates are as follows:

Statutory federal tax rate	35.0%
State taxes, net of federal tax benefit and other	5.0
Effective tax rate	40.0%

CLIENT PREPARED DRAFT FINANCIAL STATEMENTS (7/7)

Note 4. Debt Arrangements

Long-term obligations consist of the following:	(In Thousands)
12% 30 year mortgage payable, due in monthly installments until April 2026	1,736
14% 30 year mortgage payable, due in monthly installments until October 2031	883
11% 30 year mortgage payable, due in monthly installments until February 2041	642
8% 30 year mortgage payable, due in monthly installments until April 2044	1,443
	4,704
Less current maturities	38
	$ 4,666

Maturities of long-term obligations for the next five years are as follows (in thousands): 2015, $620; 2016, $620; 2017, $5,668; 2018, $620; 2019, $620; and $620 thereafter.

Short-term debt consisted of $12,800 in promissory notes issued to banks.

Note 5. Lease Commitments and Total Rental Expense

The Company leases office space, retail stores, and manufacturing facilities, under non-cancelable agreements, which expire on various dates through 2031. The leases generally provide for the lessee to pay taxes, maintenance, insurance and certain other operating costs of the leased property. Following is a summary of future minimum payments under capitalized leases and under operating leases that have initial or remaining lease terms of one year:

	Capitalized Leases (In Thousands)
Year ending December 31,2015	
Years after 2015	
Total minimum lease payments	
Imputed interest	
Present value of minimum capitalized lease payments	1,699
Current portion	403
Long-term capitalized lease obligations	$1,296

Assets recorded under capital leases are included in property, plant and equipment as follows:	
Leased buildings	$ 3,490
Accumulated depreciation	2,708
	$ 782

Note 6. Accrued Expenses

Accrued expenses are comprised of the following:	(In Thousands)
Workers' compensation insurance	$ 732
Other insurances	789
Compensation	400
Warranty	424
Advertising	357
Other	5,067
Total accrued expenses	$ 7,769

Note 7. Compensation and Benefit Agreements

To be done by West & Fair actuarial department.

CLIENT PREPARED WORKING TRIAL BALANCE (1/4)

PROLI FOOTWEAR
WORKING TRIAL BALANCE-DECEMBER 31, 2014

Accounts	Account #	Preliminary Balances Debit	Preliminary Balances Credit	--- Debit --- AJE #	Amount	--- Credit --- AJE #	Amount	Audited Balances Debit	Credit
Petty Cash	1000	3,000							
Cash-Operating Account	1010	166,083							
Cash-Payroll Account	1020	0							
Cash-Treasury Bills	1030	150,000							
Trade Accounts Receivable	1200	26,566,100							
Allowance for Doubtful Accounts	1250		1,100,000						
Other Accounts Receivable	1260	0							
Inventories: Raw Materials	1310	6,550,104							
Inventories: Work in Process	1315	0							
Inventories: Finished Goods	1320	37,117,696							
Prepaid Expenses	1400	4,717,900							
Land	1511	1,879,000							
Buildings	1512	3,464,840							
Leased Buildings	1513	3,489,988							
Manufacturing Equipment	1521	14,992,700							
Warehouse Equipment	1522	13,795,400							
Office Equipment	1523	3,539,800							
Accumulated Depreciation-Buildings	1531		3,534,647						
Accumulated Depreciation-Leased Builds	1532		2,708,170						
Accumulated Depreciation-Manu Equipment	1533		12,693,959						
Accumulated Depreciation-Warehouse Equipment	1534		4,909,542						
Accumulated Depreciation-Office Equipment	1535		1,934,198						

CLIENT PREPARED WORKING TRIAL BALANCE (2/4)

PROLI FOOTWEAR
WORKING TRIAL BALANCE - DECEMBER 31, 2014

Accounts	Account #	Preliminary Balances Debit	Preliminary Balances Credit	--- Debit --- AJE #	--- Debit --- Amount	--- Credit --- AJE #	--- Credit --- Amount	Audited Balances Debit	Audited Balances Credit
Trademarks	1540	10,129,800							
Patents	1542	1,328,400							
Goodwill	1545	8,267,700							
Accumulated Amortization - Trademarks	1550		1,463,026						
Accumulated Amortization - Patents	1552		929,608						
Accumulated Amortization - Goodwill	1555		2,765,639						
Other Assets	1600	3,284,600							
Deferred Tax Asset	1650	0							
Current Maturities of Leases	2110		403,123						
Current Maturities of Mortgages Payable	2120		37,995						
Notes Payable	2200		12,800,000						
Accounts Payable	2300		3,815,900						
Accrued Expenses	2400		7,769,300						
Interest Payable-Notes Payable	2410		0						
Interest Payable-Leases	2411		0						
Interest Payable-Mortgages Payable	2412		0						
Dividends Payable	2420		0						
Income Taxes Payable	2430		150,000						
Long Term Lease Obligations	2510		1,296,451						
Mortgages Payable	2520		4,666,003						
Deferred Compensation and Benefits	2600		3,357,200						
Deferred Income Tax Liability	2700		0						

CLIENT PREPARED WORKING TRIAL BALANCE (3/4)

PROLI FOOTWEAR
WORKING TRIAL BALANCE - DECEMBER 31, 2014

Accounts	Account #	Preliminary Balances Debit	Preliminary Balances Credit	--- Debit --- AJE #	Amount	--- Credit --- AJE #	Amount	Audited Balances Debit	Credit
Common Stock	3000		50,000						
Additional Paid in Capital	3100		22,500,000						
Retained Earnings	3200		49,966,113						
Prior Period Adjustment	3220		0						
Dividends Declared	3250	1,500,000							
Gross Sales	5000		148,235,225						
Sales Discounts	5100	372,191							
Sales Returns & Allowances	5200	1,117,535							
Cost of Goods Sold	6000	108,711,900							
Advertising and Promotion	7050	1,405,639							
Bad Debt Expense	7100	880,000							
Delivery Expense	7150	2,504,230							
Depreciation Expense-Buildings	7201	1,476,213							
Depreciation Expense-Leased Buildings	7202	310,330							
Depreciation Expense-Manu Equipment	7203	594,320							
Depreciation Expense-Warehouse Equipment	7204	714,003							
Depreciation Expense-Office Equipment	7205	306,165							
Amortization Expense - Trademarks	7230	253,108							
Amortization Expense - Patents	7232	47,356							
Amortization Expense - Goodwill	7235	859,093							

CLIENT PREPARED WORKING TRIAL BALANCE (4/4)

PROLI FOOTWEAR

WORKING TRIAL BALANCE - DECEMBER 31, 2014

Accounts	Account #	Preliminary Balances		--- Debit ---		--- Credit ---		Audited Balances	
		Debit	Credit	AJE #	Amount	AJE #	Amount	Debit	Credit
Insurance Expense	7250	501,479							
Professional Services	7300	2,079,611							
Rent Expense	7350	1,222,480							
Utilities Expense	7360	1,356,432							
Repairs and Maintenance Expense	7380	930,464							
Commissions Expense	7440	1,370,007							
Salaries Expense	7450	12,284,718							
Bonus Expense	7460	100,000							
Warranty Expense	7470	292,000							
Taxes and Licenses Expense	7500	259,050							
Telecommunications Expense	7550	2,066,900							
Travel & Entertainment Expense	7600	601,115							
Miscellaneous Expenses	7650	461,694							
Impairment Loss	7900	0							
Gain/Loss on Sale of Plant Assets	8100	0							
Interest Expense-Notes Payable	8310	1,181,006							
Interest Expense-Leases	8320	217,577							
Interest Expense-Mortgages Payable	8330	485,472							
Interest Income	8400		0						
Miscellaneous Non-Operating Income	8500		419,100						
Settlement Loss	8550	0							
Income Tax Expense	8600	1,600,000							
Unreconciled Differences	9000	0							
TOTALS		287,505,199	287,505,199						

ASSIGNMENT #1: CREATING THE PERMANENT FILE

ASSIGNMENT

1. Complete each step of the creating the permanent file audit program. Indicate completion for each step by making sure that the step is initialed, dated, and that the workpaper reference is indicated. For those audit program steps that are already initialed as having been completed, enter an appropriate date and workpaper reference next to the initials.

2. Be sure to use the appropriate tickmarks to indicate the specific work performed on each piece of audit documentation.

3. Complete and submit for grading all the audit documentation for this section and the following additional items:
   a. Audit program with dates, initials and working paper references
   b. Knowledge of company business worksheet
   c. Updated time control worksheet

AUDIT PROGRAM - CREATING THE PERMANENT FILE

Procedures	Initials	Date	W/P Ref
1. Obtain a signed engagement letter from Proli Footwear.			
a. Comply with West & Fair CPAs, LLC policy on engagement letters.	RP		
2. Read the client prepared prior year financial reports.	RP	8/x/14	
3. Review all previous year working papers.	RP		
4. Assemble initial documentation for permanent files.	RP	8/x/14	
5. Arrange with the client for such matters as adequate working space for the auditors and access to records.	RP	8/x/14	
6. Have all audit staff members review permanent file.			
a. Read permanent file document 1.1 and complete knowledge of company business worksheet.			
b. Review all legal documents.	RP	1/4-1/8/15	
c. Read minutes of all Board of Directors' meetings.	RP	1/4-1/8/15	

Engagement Letter
West & Fair, Certified Public Accountants, LLC
Stamford, Connecticut

November 14, 2013

Mr. Samuel Sole, Jr., Chairman
Proli Footwear, Inc.
Proli, Connecticut

Dear Mr. Sole:

This will confirm our understanding of the arrangements for our audit of the financial statements of Proli Footwear, Inc., for the year ending December 31, 2014.

We will audit the Company's balance sheet as of December 31, 2014, and the related statements of income, retained earnings, and especially cash flows for the year then ended, for the purpose of expressing an opinion on them. The financial statements are the responsibility of the Company management. Our responsibility is to express an opinion on the financial statements based on our audit.

We will conduct our audit in accordance with generally accepted auditing standards. Those standards require that we plan and perform the audit to obtain reasonable assurance about whether the financial statements are free of material misstatement. An audit includes examining, on a test basis, evidence supporting the amounts and disclosures in the financial statements. An audit also includes assessing the accounting principles used and significant estimates made by management, as well as evaluating the overall financial statement presentation. We believe that our audit will provide a reasonable basis for our opinion.

Our procedures will include tests of documentary evidence supporting the transactions recorded in the accounts, and direct confirmation of receivables and certain other assets and liabilities by correspondence with selected customers, creditors, legal counsel, and banks. At the conclusion of our audit, we will request certain written representations from you about the financial statements and matters related thereto.

Although the audit is designed to provide reasonable assurance of detecting errors and irregularities that are material to the financial statements, it is not designed and cannot be relied upon to disclose all fraud, defalcations, or other irregularities. However, we will inform you of any material errors, and all irregularities or illegal acts, unless they are clearly inconsequential, that come to our attention.

If you intend to publish or otherwise reproduce the financial statements and make reference to our firm, you agree to provide us with printers' proofs or masters for our review and approval before printing. You also agree to provide us with a copy of the final reproduced material for our approval before it is distributed.

Assistance to be supplied by your personnel, including the preparation of schedules and analyses of accounts, is described in a separate attachment. Timely completion of this work will facilitate the completion of our audit.

Our fees will be billed as work progresses and are based on the amount of time required plus out-of-pocket expenses. Invoices are payable upon presentation. We will notify you immediately of any circumstances we encounter that could significantly affect our initial estimate of total fees, which will range from $200,000 to $225,000.

The working papers for this engagement are the property of West & Fair, Certified Public Accountants, LLC and constitute confidential information.

If this letter correctly expresses your understanding, please sign the enclosed copy where indicated and return it to us.

We appreciate the opportunity to serve you and trust that our association will be a long and pleasant one.

Sincerely yours,
West & Fair, Certified Public Accountants, LLC
Patricia Fair, CPA
Patricia Fair, CPA,
Managing Partner

Accepted by: *Samuel Sole, Jr.*   Date: *November 18, 2013*

Permanent File - Document List

Document Number	Description
(PF1.1)	Company history and operational information
(PF1.2)	Minutes of Board of Directors' meetings
(PF2.1)	Asset Purchase Agreement, dated as of April 22, 2010, between Proli Footwear, Inc. and Dapper Manufacturing Co.
(PF2.2)	Asset Purchase Agreement, dated February 13, 2012, by and among Mudhoppers Inc. and Proli Footwear, Inc.
(PF3.1)	Restated Articles of Incorporation of Proli Footwear, Inc.
(PF3.2)	Bylaws of Proli Footwear, Inc., as amended to date
(PF4.1)	Credit Agreement, dated as of May 31, 2012 by and among Proli Footwear, Inc. and CT National Bank
(PF5.1)	Employment Agreement, dated as of April 26, 2004 between Proli Footwear, Inc. and Goodwin Buye.
(PF5.2)	Employment Agreement, dated as of June 25, 2008, and amended as of August 7, 2009, and December 31, 2010 between Josephine Chopines and Proli Footwear, Inc.
(PF5.3)	Employment Agreement, dated as of November 19, 2013 between Proli Footwear, Inc. and Harold F. Heele.
(PF5.4)	Employment Agreement, dated as of January 14, 2008, and amended as of January 25, 2010 between Proli Footwear, Inc. and Samuel Sole, III.
(PF5.5)	Employment Agreement, dated as of January 2, 2014 between Verna F. Vamp and Proli Footwear, Inc.
(PF6.1)	Proli Footwear, Inc. Retirement Plan
(PF6.2)	Proli Footwear, Inc. Employees' Retirement Savings Plan
(PF7.1)	Agreement, dated as of April 20, 2014, between United Steel Workers of America, AFL-CIO, and Proli Footwear, Inc.
(PF7.2)	Agreement, dated as of May 5, 2013 between International Ladies Garment Workers Union and Proli Footwear, Inc.
(PF8.1)	Lease, dated as of February 28, 2011, between Walton Properties and Proli Footwear, Inc.
(PF8.2)	Lease, dated as of May 28, 2001, between Proli Rental Properties and Proli Footwear, Inc.
(PF8.3)	Lease, dated as of May 28, 2001, between Alice Fair Real Estate Associates and Proli Footwear, Inc.
(PF8.4)	Lease, dated as of July 28, 2006 between Proli Rental Properties and Proli Footwear, Inc.
(PF8.5)	Lease, dated as of August 28, 2012, between Alice Fair Real Estate Associates and Proli Footwear, Inc.
(PF8.6)	Lease, dated as of January 1, 2014, between Proli Rental Properties and Proli Footwear, Inc.
(PF9.1)	Trademark License, dated as of July 7, 2011 between Dryer Industries, Inc. and Dapper Manufacturing Co.
(PF10.1)	Prior year summary financial statements
(PF10.2)	December 31, 2013 West & Fair opening balance audit documentation.

Document PF1.1

Company History and Operational Information

Proli ("Proli") Footwear, Inc. was founded by Samuel Sole, Sr. and was incorporated in Connecticut in 1941. Samuel Sole, Sr.'s five children now own Proli. The Company is planning to go public within the next five years and has hired an independent accounting firm, West & Fair CPAs, LLC to assist in preparing the company and its financial employees for this undertaking.

Proli designs, develops, engineers, manufactures, markets, and distributes branded premium quality protective footwear for the sporting, outdoor, and occupational markets. Proli products feature innovative yet classic design, functional performance and durability, and are relatively unaffected by changing fashion designs. The company believes that this combination distinguishes its brands and makes them an outstanding value. The company markets its products primarily through an employee sales force and also through selected distributors. It also manufactures private label footwear and footwear components. The company's primary SIC code is 3143.

Historically, Proli has mainly produced premium sporting and recreational leather boots. In April 2010, the Company acquired the business of Dapper Manufacturing Co., a producer of premium quality leather footwear for the sporting market, which is sold primarily under the Dapper® brand. In February 2012, the Company purchased the assets of Mudhoppers Inc. to broaden the base of business in the weather-protective footwear area. Mudhoppers designs and markets protective footwear and raingear that is sold primarily under the Mudhoppers® brand. The operations of Mudhoppers have been included in the Company's financial statements since the date of acquisition. In July 2012 the Company acquired the operating assets and trademarks of Softshoe Inc. Softshoe historically sold footwear primarily of rubber or vinyl, some of which includes leather or fabric uppers. In July 2013 the Company acquired all of the outstanding shares of Woodland Corporation, the company that operated under the Woodland® trade name. Woodland is a designer, manufacturer and marketer of branded leather footwear for the outdoor market.

Products

The Company's brand product offering includes these major categories:

> *Leather Footwear*
> The majority of the products sold by the Company is leather footwear marketed under four brand names, Leatherworker®, Proli®, Woodland®, and Dapper®. The Proli® products consist of premium quality sporting, occupational and recreational boots available in numerous styles. The Leatherworker® brand markets a broad line of utility, steel toe and sporting boots and recreational hikers. The Woodland® and Dapper® consist of a focused line of indoor and outdoor work boots appealing to consumers who desire durability and comfort.
>
> *Rubber/Vinyl Footwear*
> The Company's rubber/vinyl footwear line is extensive with product offerings covering the sporting, recreational and occupational markets. The Company markets rubber/vinyl footwear mainly under the Sportech® and Litetech® brands. The product line ranges from low cost vinyl molded products to high performance, hand-crafted rubber products directed to specific occupational market niches.
>
> *Protective Footwear*
> Mudhoppers® offers a broad line of quality raingear and protective footwear appealing to those workers in utility, construction, law enforcement and other groups traditionally purchasing through industrial distributors. The Mudhoppers® brand is recognized in the industry for its durability, quality and heritage.

Product Design and Development

Product design and development ideas are initiated both internally by the Company's development staff and externally by customers and suppliers. Consumers, sales personnel and suppliers work closely to identify opportunities for new styles, design improvements and new materials. The Company's marketing division interacts with the product development department during the development and testing of new products. The Company's pattern, design and chemistry lab staffs address new product needs that are related to functional or technical characteristics. Marketing personnel, at times in conjunction with outside design consultants, determine the final aesthetics of the product. Once a product design is approved for production, responsibility shifts to manufacturing for pattern development and commercialization.

Customers, Sales and Distribution

The Company markets its brands and associated products through two separate channels of distribution: retail and industrial.

Within the retail market, the products are marketed through a sales force comprised of 25 Company employed sales people and seven independent sales representative groups. A national account sales team complements the sales activities for all the brands. Historically, the independent sales representatives make approximately 32% of the Company's sales; they are paid commissions at the rate of 3% of gross sales.

The Company's industrial products are distributed through the Leatherworker Division using a combination of Company employed field sales persons, independent representatives and a national account team.

The Company's products are sold directly to more than 1,500 accounts, including sporting goods/outdoor retailers, general merchandise and independent shoe stores, wholesalers, industrial distributors, catalog operations and the United States government. The Company's customer base is also diversified as to size and location of customer and markets served. As a result, the Company is not dependent upon a few customers, and adverse economic conditions or mild or dry weather conditions in a specific region are less likely to have a material effect on the Company's results of operations.

The Company operates one factory outlet store whose primary purpose is disposal of slow moving, factory seconds and obsolete merchandise. The store is located at the Proli, CT manufacturing facility. Sales in the factory outlet store are approximately 3% of the Company's total sales each year.

Advertising and Promotion

Because a majority of the Company's marketing expenditures are for promotional materials, cooperative advertising and point-of-sale advertising designed to assist dealers and distributors in the sale of the Company's products, the Company is able to customize advertising and marketing for each of its brands in each of its distribution channels. The Company's marketing strategy allows it to emphasize those features of its products that have special appeal to the applicable targeted consumer.

The Company advertises and promotes its products through a variety of methods including national and regional print advertising, public relations, point-of-sale displays, catalogs and packaging.

The Company participates in several charity programs. Each year it donates 500 pairs of leather work boots to the Connecticut Winter Clothing Program that distributes warm clothing to those in need during the cold winter months. Proli also contributes premium leather footwear to the Connecticut Public Television Charity Auction. The Company participates in several other charity functions throughout the year. These activities have made Proli Footwear a well-known product and business in the state. Charitable contribution expenses are recorded in the miscellaneous expenses account (# 7650) and generally do not exceed $50,000 in any given year.

Manufacturing

The Company manufactures its footwear in the United States because the Company believes it is able to maintain better control over quality, inventory production scheduling and inventory levels. "Made in the USA" is prominently displayed in the Company's advertising, promotion and marketing materials. The Company's manufacturing facilities are located in Proli, CT, Waterbury, CT and Walton, FL. A majority of its rubber, leather and vinyl products are produced in these three facilities. Leather tops and liners for the Sportech® and Litetech® brands and some leather boots are produced at the Company's Walton, FL facility.

Suppliers

The Company uses three principal raw materials in its production process: leather, crude rubber and oil based vinyl compounds for vinyl footwear. While the Company saw price increases during 2011 for all three of these raw materials, prices have since stabilized at lower levels and the Company has no reason to believe that all three of these raw materials will not continue to be available at competitive prices. The Company also uses technical components in the Company's products including THINER®, DRYTEX®, CORDY®, ICETEC®, and VINYLAM®. No interruption in the supply of any of these components is anticipated.

The Company's Softshoe Inc. Division purchases DRYTEX® waterproof fabric directly from Dryer Industries ("Dryer"), for both Sportech® and Litetech® brand footwear. Dryer has traditionally been Softshoe's single largest supplier, in terms of dollars spent on raw materials. Approximately 9% of Proli's footwear, in terms of number of pairs produced, incorporates DRYTEX® waterproof fabric. Agreements with Dryer may be terminated by either party upon 60 days' written notice. The Company considers its relationship with Dryer to be good. Effective January 1, 2013 the majority of Softshoe's DRYTEX® footwear is guaranteed to be waterproof for one year from the date of purchase compared to two years previously.

Quality Assurance

The Company's quality control programs are important to its reputation for manufacturing superior footwear. The Company is currently in the process of becoming ISO 14001 certified, with certification planned for the fourth quarter of 2015.

The Company's Proli, CT plant has a chemistry lab that is responsible for the testing of incoming raw materials and work-in process. All crude rubber is tested to assure that each batch meets the high values specified by the Company for range of plasticity and rate of cure, both of which have a direct relationship to the ultimate quality of the product. Fabrics are sample tested to meet Proli's requirements for strength and weight. Incoming leather skins are inspected for color, grade and weight.

The Company's Softshoe operation tests 100% of all DRYTEX® bootie liners for leaks prior to sewing them into boots. Approximately 1% of all completed waterproof boots are filled with water for testing. Leather is tested for lasting ability, tear strength, finish and thickness.

Warranty

The Company offers a one year limited warranty on all products. Any defective product can be returned within one year of purchase and a replacement will be sent with no shipping charge.

Backlog

At December 31, 2014, the Company had unfilled orders from its customers in the amount of approximately $33.7 million compared to $34.2 million at December 31, 2013. The decrease in backlog is primarily the result of a consumer rainwear order from a large mass merchant that was included in the December 31, 2013 backlog. All orders at December 31, 2014 are expected to be filled during 2015. Because a major portion of the Company's orders are placed in January through July for delivery in June through October, the Company's backlog is lowest during the fourth quarter and peaks during the second quarter. Factors other than seasonality, such as pending large national account orders or United States government orders, could have a significant impact on the Company's backlog. Therefore, backlog at any one point in time may not be indicative of future results. Generally, orders may be canceled by customers prior to shipment without penalty.

Competition

The Company's various categories of footwear are marketed in a competitive environment. The Company competes with numerous manufacturers (domestic and foreign) and importers of footwear, many of whom have substantially greater financial, distribution and marketing resources than the Company. Because the Company has a broad product line, its competition varies by product category. The Company has two to three major domestic competitors in most of its rubber and vinyl product lines, at least four major competitors in connection with the Company's sporting footwear, at least six major competitors in connection with hiking boots and at least four major competitors in connection with its occupational footwear. The Company also faces competition from offshore manufacturers, particularly in the occupational market.

Proli believes it maintains a competitive position compared to its competitors through its attention to quality and the delivery of value, its position as an innovator in common product segments, its above average record of delivering products on a timely basis, its strong customer relationships and, in some cases, the breadth of its product line. Some of the Company's competitors compete mainly on the basis of price.

Employees

As of December 31, 2014, the Company had approximately 1,500 employees, all located in the United States. Approximately 600 of the Company's employees at the Proli, CT facility are represented by the United Steel Workers of America under a three-year collective bargaining agreement which expires in May 2017, approximately 250 of the Company's employees at the Waterbury, CT facility are represented by the United Food & Commercial Workers Union under a collective bargaining agreement which expires in September 2018 and approximately 85 of the Company's employees at the Walton, FL facility are represented by the International Ladies Garment Workers Union under a collective bargaining agreement which expires in January 2016.

Foreign Operations and Export Sales

The Company does not have any foreign operations. International sales accounted for less than 5% of the Company's net sales in 2014.

Seasonality

As has traditionally been the case, the Company's sales in 2014 were higher in the last two quarters of the year than in the first two quarters and, in order to satisfy shipping requirements, the Company builds inventory during the first half of the year and offers customers price discounts and extended terms during such time. The Company expects these trends to continue.

Trademarks, Tradenames and Patents

The Company owns United States federal registrations for several of its marks, including Proli®, Dapper®, Leatherworker®, Litetech®, Mudhoppers®, Sportech®, and Woodland®. The Company does not believe any trademark is material to its business.

Prior to 2014, the Company paid a royalty on sales of products carrying the Dapper® name equal to 0.5% of the price of products sold that applies to net sales in excess of $4.0 million annually. The royalty agreement expired on December 31, 2013. The Company is not aware of any material conflicts concerning its marks or its use of marks owned by other companies.

The Company owns several patents that improve its competitive position in the marketplace. The Company is not aware of any infringement of its patents or that it is infringing any patents owned by third parties.

Environmental Matters

The Company and the industry in which it competes are subject to environmental laws and regulations concerning emissions to the air, discharges to waterways and the generation, handling, storage, transportation, treatment and disposal of waste materials. The Company's policy is to comply with all applicable environmental, health and safety laws and regulations. These laws and regulations are constantly evolving and it is difficult to predict accurately the effect they will have on the Company in the future. Compliance with applicable environmental regulations and controls has not had, nor are they expected to have in 2015, any material impact on the capital expenditures, earnings or competitive position of the Company.

Properties

The following table sets forth information, as of December 31, 2014, relating to the Company's principal facilities:

Property Location	Owned or Leased	Approximate Floor Area (square feet)	Principal Uses
Proli, CT	Leased	178,000	Principal sales, marketing and executive offices and warehouse space
Proli, CT	Owned	385,000	Manufacture leather and rubber footwear
Proli, CT	Leased	350,000	Main warehouse and distribution facility
Proli, CT	Owned	8,000	Retail outlet store
Walton, FL	Owned	62,500	Manufacture leather components and construct rubber boots
Walton, FL	Owned	250,000	Manufacture injection molded products
Walton, FL	Leased	89,000	Warehouse and distribution facility
Waterbury, CT	Leased	125,000	Warehouse and distribution facility
Waterbury, CT	Leased	94,700	Manufacturing, warehousing and offices for Mudhoppers, Inc

Key Employees

The following table sets forth information, as of December 31, 2014, regarding the employees and officers of the Company:

Name	Age	Position
Samuel Sole, Jr.	75	Chairman of the Board and Director
Josephine Chopines	52	President, Chief Executive Officer and Director
Goodwin Buye	47	Vice President - Purchasing
Harold F. Heele	49	Vice President - Finance and Administration and Chief Financial Officer
Samuel Sole, III	53	Vice President - Product Development
Verna F. Vamp	40	Vice President - Information Technology
Brian Baddude	34	Controller

The term of office of each of the executive officers expires at the annual meeting of directors.

- Samuel Sole, Jr. was elected to the Board of Directors in 1979. Since 1998, Mr. Sole also has served as Chairman of the Board of the Company.
- Josephine Chopines has served as President, Chief Executive Officer and as a director of the Company since December 31, 2010. Prior thereto, Ms. Chopines served as Executive Vice President and Chief Operating Officer of the Company since August 2009 and as Executive Vice President since June 2008. From March 1999, when she joined the Company, until June 2008, Ms. Chopines was Vice President Finance.
- Goodwin Buye joined the Company in 1990 and has held various positions in finance and administration since that time. In April 2004, Mr. Buye was elected Vice President - Purchasing.
- Harold F. Heele joined the Company in 2013. Previously Mr. Heele was employed for ten years as the Vice President of Finance for a publicly-traded footwear company.
- Samuel Sole, III joined the Company in January 2006 as a territory salesperson. In January 2007, Mr. Sole was appointed the National Accounts Manager. He served in such capacity until January 2008 when he was appointed Senior Marketing Manager, and in January 2010 he was elected Vice President – Product Development.
- Verna F. Vamp has served as Vice President - Information Technology since she joined the Company in January 2014. Prior to this, Ms. Vamp was an independent information systems consultant.
- Samuel Sole, III is the son of Samuel Sole, Jr. None of the other directors or executive officers are related to each other.
- Brian Baddude is the grandson of Vanda Sole, Samuel Sole, Jr.'s sister and a shareholder of the Company. Brian is responsible for the general ledger and various financial reporting control functions. Mr. Baddude joined the Company in 2011 as assistant controller. In 2013, he was promoted to controller. Mr. Baddude graduated with an MBA from the Jackson Grand Teton State University in 2009.

As a standard pre-audit procedure, West and Fair, CPAs, LLC conducted a background investigation of key Company personnel before accepting an audit engagement. The objective is to identify any problems or situations that may have a negative effect on the business environment of the Company and the outcome of the audit. The following information was extracted from the investigation report based on the review by the partners for consideration by the audit team members as they undertake the planning and conduct of the audit:

1. Samuel Sole Jr.'s net worth is estimated to be approximately $25-30 million. He lives on Candleweed Lake (Proli section of lake) in a home valued at approximately $2.5 million. There is no mortgage on his home. He has been a widower for about 5 years.

2. Goodwin Buye (known as GB to his friends) also lives in the Streamfield section of Candleweed Lake with his wife, the former Joanna (Joan) Scuff, in a house valued at about $2.2 million. There is and no mortgage on the property. Accurate net worth information for Mr. Buye was not available, but it is believed that he and his wife have a net worth in excess of $6.0 million. His wife Joan holds an MBA from Fairhill University and is known as a successful business woman with a number of entrepreneurial interests.

3. Verna Vamp lives in Newcity, Connecticut in a house valued at about $600,000 with an outstanding mortgage of $150,000. She has been divorced from her former husband Howard Vamp for about 7 years. Howard Vamp is Harold Heele's first cousin. Ms. Vamp's net worth is approximately $900,000. It is rumored that she has a "relationship" with Brian Baddude. They have been observed in public together from time to time. No conclusion is possible about this suspected relationship at this time.

4. Brian Baddude lives in Old Milford, CT with his wife, the former Jeana Beana in a house valued at $650,000 with an outstanding mortgage of approximately $400,000. His net worth is estimated to be approximately $500,000.

Legal Proceedings

The Company is involved in two lawsuits.

1. In a federal lawsuit, the Company has been cited as a potentially responsible party in the dumping of toxic waste into the Housatonic River. The government is asserting remediation costs of $1.3 million.

2. On June 25, 2014, a worker at a construction site in Podunk, IL was injured when he tripped and fell at the site. The worker is asserting that the heel of his Leatherman® shoe was defective and broke. This worker has sustained disabling leg and foot injuries and is unable to return to work. Economic damages in the amount of $2.8 million are being sought.

From time to time, the Company, in the normal course of business, is also involved in various other claims and legal actions arising out of its operations. The Company does not believe that the ultimate disposition of any currently pending claims or actions would have a material adverse effect on the Company or its financial condition.

Document PF10.1

Prior Year Summary Financial Statements

PROLI FOOTWEAR, INC.
BALANCE SHEETS
DECEMBER 31,

ASSETS	2013 (000)	2012 (000)
Current Assets:		
Cash	$469	$7,388
Accounts Receivable	31,889	24,426
Allowance for Doubtful Accts	(1,760)	(1,650)
Inventories	42,980	34,704
Prepaid Expenses	5,137	4,418
Total Current Assets	78,715	69,286
Property, Plant & Equipment, net	14,589	14,081
Other Assets	18,809	18,149
Total Assets	$112,113	$101,516
LIABILITIES & EQUITY		
Current Liabilities	$24,874	$16,747
Long-Term Obligations	18,619	22,193
Shareholders' Equity	68,620	62,576
Total Liabilities & Equity	$112,113	$101,516

PROLI FOOTWEAR, INC.
INCOME STATEMENTS
YEAR ENDED DECEMBER 31,

	2013 (000)	2012 (000)
	Except per share amounts	
Net Sales	$160,053	$134,197
Cost of Goods Sold	(115,161)	(96,994)
Gross Profit	44,892	37,203
Selling & Administrative Expenses	(30,421)	(26,106)
Operating Income	14,472	11,097
Non-Operating Income(Expense)		
Interest Expense	(2,247)	(1,848)
Other	279	460
Income before Taxes	12,504	9,709
Income TaxExpense	(5,047)	(3,784)
Net Income	$7,457	$5,925
Earnings Per Share	$149.14	$118.50

Note 1: 50,000 shares were outstanding for 2012 and 2013.
Note 2: Dividends per share in 2012 and 2013 were $40.00.

Document PF10.2 (1/5)

AUDIT MEMO
West & Fair CPAs, LLC
Stamford, CT

Re: Proli Footwear
Inventory Observation and Audit Procedures Performed
December 31, 2013

I was present during the physical inventory count on January 2, 2014 at the Proli, CT facilities.

I made test counts of the client's shoe inventory on hand at January 2, 2014 (see attached schedule Z-4).

I made test counts of supplies on hand at January 2, 2014 and traced these counts to the client's summary sheets.

The client stopped production on 12/19/2013. There was no work-in-progress noted in the factory or warehouse. The last 5 receiving reports issued in 2013 are as follows:

Z-7	#841 on 12/26 from Aukland Leather
Z-7	#842 on 12/26 from Elfriede's Famous Fabrics
Z-7	#843 on 12/26 from Vijay Vinyl Supply
Z-7	#844 on 12/29 from Scuff Leather
Z-7	#845 on 12/30 from Indio's Rubber Supply

I examined all these items and determined that they were included in the physical inventory count. No receiving reports have been issued since 12/30/2013.

I traced all inventory test counts from all facilities to the client's physical inventory tag control (Z-4, Z-5, Z-6). I then traced the information from the tag control to the count sheet summary. On a test basis, I traced items from the count sheet summary to the inventory tag control. On a test basis, I vouched the unit costs to recent invoices.

Z-2
VN 1/3/14

AUDIT MEMO
West & Fair CPAs, LLC
Stamford, CT

Re: Proli Footwear
Inventory Observation
December 31, 2013

I was present during the physical inventory count on January 2, 2013 at the Waterbury, CT facilities.

I made test counts of the client's shoe inventory on hand at January 2, 2013 (see attached schedule Z-5). I made test counts of supplies on hand at January 2, 2013 and traced these counts to the client's summary sheets. On a test basis, I traced items from the count sheet summary to the inventory tag control.

The client stopped production on 12/19/2013. There was no work-in-progress noted in the factory or warehouse. No receiving reports have been issued since 12/30/2013.

···

Z-3
EP 1/3/14

AUDIT MEMO
West & Fair CPAs, LLC
Stamford, CT

Re: Proli Footwear
Inventory Observation
December 31, 2013

I was present during the physical inventory count on January 2, 2014 at the Walton, FL facilities.

I made test counts of the client's shoe inventory on hand at January 2, 2014 (see attached schedule Z-6). I made test counts of supplies on hand at January 2, 2014 and traced these counts to the client's summary sheets. On a test basis, I traced items from the count sheet summary to the inventory tag control.

The client stopped production on 12/19/2013. There was no work-in-progress noted in the factory or warehouse. No receiving reports have been issued since 12/30/2013.

Z-4
RP 1/2/14

Proli Footwear
Inventory Test Counts –
Proli, CT Location
December 31, 2013

Tag #	Item Description		Count
104	Proli A	T	13,284
138	Icetemp	T	21,224
114	Dapper	T	9,052
121	Proli A	T	199
105	Litetech	T	6,578
136	Icetemp	T	9,124
143	Sportech	T	9,745
118	Woodland	T	35,249

Z-5
VN 1/2/14 RP 1/9/14

Proli Footwear
Inventory Test Counts –
Waterbury, CT Location
December 31, 2013

Tag #	Item Description		Count
228	Mudhoppers	T	10,750
201	Icetemp	T	24,038

Z-6
EP 1/2/14 RP 1/9/14

Proli Footwear
Inventory Test Counts –
Walton, FL Location
December 31, 2013

Tag #	Item Description		Count
333	Leatherworker	T	35,553
301	Litetech	T	35,676
329	Leatherworker	T	19,689

T – Traced to physical inventory tag control

15

Proli Footwear
Purchase Cut-Off Analysis
December 31, 2013

Receiving Report #	Receiving Report Date	Received from		Inventory #1310	Freight-In #6400	Accounts Payable #2300	Purchase Journal Date	Comments	Auditor Action
Z-1 841	12/26/13	Aukland Leather	∨	75,453	307	75,760	12/29/13	Shipped FOB destination on 12/1/13	None
Z-1 842	12/26/13	Elfriede's Famous Fabric	∨	65,461	197	65,658	12/29/13	Shipped FOB destination on 12/19/13	None
Z-1 843	12/26/13	Vijay Vinyl Supply	∨	28,568	58	28,626	12/30/13	Shipped FOB shipping point on 12/14/13	None
Z-1 844	12/29/13	Scuff GB Leather	∨	35,589	67	35,656	12/30/13	Shipped FOB shipping point on 12/10/13	None
Z-1 845	12/30/13	Indio's Rubber Supply	∨	7,623	34	7,657	12/30/13	Shipped FOB destination on 12/22/13	None
846	1/5/14	Vinyl Magic	∨	19,449	37	19,486	1/6/14	Shipped FOB shipping point on 12/24/13	Purchase belongs in 2013 - AJE #1
847	1/6/14	Formal Fabrics	∨	28,754	186	28,940	1/6/14	Shipped FOB destination on 12/29/13	None
848	1/6/14	Marie's Supplies	∨	54,019	488	54,507	1/6/14	Shipped FOB shipping point on 12/29/13	None
849	1/8/14	Veritech Adhesives	∨	84,358	1,931	86,289	1/9/14	Shipped FOB shipping point on 1/2/14	None
850	1/8/14	Vinyl Magic	∨	7,093	24	7,117	1/9/14	Shipped FOB destination on 12/30/13	None

∨ = Vouched information to original invoice

AJE #1

Inventory   19,486
    Accounts Payable   19,486

16

© Proctor and Poli

Proli Footwear
Sales Cut-off Analysis
December 31, 2013

Date	Customer	Account Number	Invoice Number	Cash #1010	Accounts Receivable #1200	Delivery Expense #7150	Sales #5000	Sales Returns & Allowances #5200	Product Cost	Comments	Auditor Action
12/29/13	Athletic Fit Shoes for Toe	27101	✓2386		18281	581	17,700		13,604	Shipped FOB shipping point on 12/28/13	None
12/29/13	All	27172	✓2387		34571	134	34,437		26,416	Shipped FOB shipping point on 12/29/13	None
12/30/13	Poppers	27180	✓2388		22,118	484	21,634		16,058	Shipped FOB shipping point on 12/29/13	None
12/30/13	Charlene's Chopines	27120	✓2389		(2,110)			(2,110)	1,565	credit memo sent to customer	None
12/31/13	Pat's Poulaines	27158	✓2390		8,999	158	8,841		6,708	Shipped FOB shipping point on 12/29/13	None
12/31/13	Walking Well	27184	✓2391		15,284	363	14,921		11,089	Shipped FOB destination on 12/30/13	Sale belongs in 2014 – AJE#2
1/5/14	Bobbi's Boots	27104	✓2392	8,066		164	7,902		5,885	Shipped FOB destination on 1/5/14	None
1/5/14	Miracle Heel	27153	✓2393		18,213	458	17,755		13,701	Shipped FOB shipping point on 1/5/14	None
1/5/14	Sal's Soles	27170	✓2394		24,565	319	24,246		17,407	Shipped FOB shipping point on 1/5/14	None
1/6/14	Zelda's	27219	✓2395		21,730	450	21,280		16,168	Shipped FOB shipping point on 1/5/14	None
1/6/14	Paradise of Pumps	27157	✓2396		5,283	367	4,916		3,658	Shipped FOB shipping point on 1/6/14	None

✓ = Vouched to invoice copy and shipping records.

AJE #12

Sales	14,921
Delivery Expense	363
Accounts Receivable	15,284

Inventory	11,089
Cost of Goods Sold	11,089

Proli Footwear
Knowledge of Company Business Worksheet
December 31, 2014

Directions: Answer **True** or **False** to each of the following questions.

		ANSWER
1.	All Proli products are produced in Connecticut.	
2.	Proli is a family-owned business.	
3.	The Chairman of the Board is also the President of Proli.	
4.	Customers help to determine the types of products that Proli sells.	
5.	One of Proli's products is raingear.	
6.	Proli only sells its products in Proli company stores.	
7.	The backlog of sales orders peaks during the period, April 1 through June 30.	
8.	The company has a labor union contract with the Teamsters.	
9.	Mudhoppers is one of Proli's registered trade names.	
10.	Proli's main marketing strategy involves the use of television advertising featuring famous athletes.	
11.	Proli has more male officers than female officers.	
12.	The company has three warehouse and distribution facilities: two in CT and one in Walton, FL.	
13.	Proli owns all its facilities.	
14.	Proli instituted a legal proceeding against the US government seeking a refund of amounts previously paid to the IRS.	
15.	Drytex® is a raw material used by Proli.	
16.	Proli has several competitors and therefore competes by its attention to product quality and value.	
17.	Sales peak in the first quarter of the calendar year for Proli.	
18.	More than half of the company's sales are to companies located outside the United States.	
19.	No company officers are related to each other.	
20.	The primary product sold by Proli is leather footwear.	
21.	Proli has had an employee stock incentive plan since 1994.	
22.	All of Proli's products are produced in the US.	
23.	Goodwin Buye is not married.	

Proli Footwear
Time Control
December 31, 2014

Section	Budgeted Time	Time Spent Working with Team	Time Spent Working Alone
1. Creating the Permanent File	3 hours		

Team member names:

ASSIGNMENT #2: PLANNING THE AUDIT

ASSIGNMENT:

1. Complete each step of the planning the audit audit program. Indicate completion for each step by making sure that the step is initialed, dated, and that the workpaper reference is indicated. For those audit program steps that are already initialed as having been completed, enter an appropriate date and workpaper reference next to the initials.

2. Be sure to use the appropriate tickmarks to indicate the specific work performed on each piece of audit documentation.

3. Complete and submit for grading all the audit documentation for this section organized in the following sequence:
   a. Audit program with dates, initials and audit documentation references;
   b. Planning memo; and
   c. Updated Time Control Worksheet.

AUDIT PROGRAM – PLANNING THE AUDIT

Procedures	Initials	Date	W/P Ref
General			
1. Meet client personnel and tour all facilities.	RP	8/14	
2. Interview Proli Footwear personnel to become familiar with operating procedures. From your notes, prepare a description of the essential operating procedures. Be sure all significant systems have been documented.	RP		
3. From the narrative of operating procedures, prepare flowcharts as the procedures exist and the documents flow at the present time.	RP		
4. Prepare a list of internal control weaknesses observed by reviewing the flowcharts and operating procedures.			
5. Coordinate the assistance of Proli personnel in data preparation and PBC schedules.	RP	8/14	
6. Establish the timing of the audit work.	RP	8/14	
7. Review audit timeline for appropriate scheduling of audit work.			
8. Establish and coordinate staffing requirements.			
Analytical			
9. Prepare a vertical analysis of the balance sheet and income statement for the current year.			

Procedures	Initials	Date	W/P Ref

10. Perform an analytic review.

    a. Calculate ratios for 2014, 2013, and 2012.

    b. Comment on any significant or unusual trends.

    c. Obtain industry ratios for 2014.   RP   1/4-1/8/15

    d. Compare to the Company's current year ratios and comment on any significant or unusual differences.

Other

11. Prepare an appraisal of audit risk.

    a. Assess the risk of material errors and irregularities.

    b. Assess audit risk

12. Determine the planning materiality, tolerable misstatement and testing threshold for individually significant items.

13. Review the "Brainstorming Session" memo.

14. Prepare the audit planning memo.

15. Prepare a written audit program. (In practice, sections of the program may be prepared or updated throughout the audit.)   RP

HELPFUL HINTS FROM THE IN-CHARGE ACCOUNTANT:

1. Use a tickmark to show each work procedure performed.

2. Refer to an audit text and read about audit planning and risk assessment.

3. Remember that any work RP has completed need not be repeated by you. You may assume that RP has done <u>all</u> the necessary work to complete the work program step correctly. *All of RP's work looks like this.*

OPERATING PROCEDURES

General Financial Reporting

All accounting systems are centralized in the Proli, CT headquarters facility. All facilities follow the same procedures. Customer checks are sent to the Proli, CT office and all vendor invoices are sent to the Proli, CT office. The Proli, CT main warehouse distribution center, processes all customer returns. At the end of each business day, the Walton, FL and Waterbury, CT facilities send all accounting documentation via National Delivery Service to the Proli, CT headquarters. All bank statements are sent to the controller's office in Proli, CT. A petty cash fund is maintained only at the Proli, CT offices.

The company's accounting software allows the use of several special journals and subsidiary ledgers. Different departments within the company update each journal. The sales journal and accounts receivable subsidiary ledger are updated by the accounts receivable billing clerk.[1] The cash receipts journal is maintained by the cashier. The cash disbursements journal is maintained by the purchasing agent. There are separate raw materials perpetual inventory ledgers for each manufacturing facility. The raw material warehouse clerk at each facility maintains them. The finished goods warehouse clerk at each warehouse facility maintains the finished goods perpetual inventory ledgers. On a daily basis the clerk in the controller's department records nonrecurring journal entries as transactions occur.

At month end copies of the journals and subsidiary ledgers are received by the controller's department and filed by month. The controller approves month-end adjusting and correcting entries by initialing them and the clerk then enters the journal entries into the system. The clerk then prints a trial balance and financial statements. The controller then reviews the statements and distributes them to the president and other members of the management team.

Sales

Customer orders are faxed in daily by the sales force. The customer calls in retail sales to the sales department. Prices to be charged are determined by reference to an approved price list. A daily listing of sales by customer is generated at the end of the day and sent to the sales manager, S. Harte Selling, who approves the listing and returns it to the sales staff. Credit is automatically granted to previous customers, whereas first-time customers must receive credit approval from the sales manager. Ninety-five percent of sales are credit sales.

A sales clerk then authorizes the system to generate a five-part sales order:

- Copy 1 goes to the customer to confirm the order
- Copy 2 is sent to the sales manager to compile sales data
- Copies 3, 4, and 5 authorize shipment or customer pickup and are sent to the shipping department, in the distribution center, to prepare the shipment

After the order is filled, Copy 3 of the sales order form is sent back to accounts receivable for billing purposes and to ensure that out of stock items are not billed to the customer. Sometimes, the accounts receivable billing clerk inadvertently bills the customer for the complete order, including backordered items. Copy 3 is then filed by customer in the accounts receivable billing department. Copy 3 is destroyed at the time of the sale for cash sales.

Over-the counter sales are also made to local customers directly out of the warehouse. All documentation for these sales is prepared in the warehouse and periodically sent to the accounts receivable billing department for posting to customer accounts. Charge tickets are the source document for charge sales and cash and checks are the source document for cash sales. The charge tickets are entered into the accounting system and filed by customer. After the cash sales are posted, the accounts receivable billing clerk sends the cash and checks to the controller's office for deposit.

Customer statements are prepared each month, immediately following the last posting of the month. A receptionist picks up customer statements from the billing clerk, prepares the mailing, and sends them to the post office by courier. Prior to the mailing, the sales manager reviews each statement to ensure that unusually large balances are investigated.

Sales Returns

Customers who want to return inventory to the company must receive prior permission from the sales manager. A sales clerk prepares a four-part return authorization.

- Copies 1 and 2 go to the customer (one copy is to be returned with the goods)
- Copy 3 goes to the receiving department to alert them to the future delivery
- Copy 4 is sent to accounts receivable-billing and filed by customer

When the goods are received, the receiving department stamps Copy 3 of the return authorization as "goods received" and forwards Copy 3 to the sales department. The sales manager then authorizes and prepares a two-part credit memorandum. No other means of reducing accounts receivable are authorized.

- Copy 1 goes to the customer
- Copy 2 goes to accounts receivable with Copy 3 of the return authorization

The accounts receivable billing clerk then matches the documents with Copy 4 of the return authorization and enters the information into the accounting system and files the complete package by customer.

Customer Order Filling

The warehouse receives Copies 3, 4, and 5 of the sales order form and fills the order as quickly as possible. The shipping clerk checks the number of units of finished goods available. Items not in stock are noted on the copies as "out of stock" and Copy 3 is sent back to accounts receivable.

Copies 4 and 5 stay with the deliver and serve as the shipping order. The delivery driver takes both copies of the shipping order. Upon delivery to the customer, the driver has the customer sign Copy 4 of the sales order form as a receipt. The driver returns this copy to the inventory clerk in the warehouse. The customer retains Copy 5 of the sales order.

Over the counter sales to local customers are handled by any available warehouse employee who takes and fills these orders at the counter. Customers pay either by check or cash, or charge the purchase to their accounts. In the case of charges, charge tickets are prepared. The cash, checks and charge tickets are kept in a file and are periodically delivered to the accounts receivable billing bookkeeper.

Cash Receipts

Customer payments and the remittance advices are received in the controller's office. Any available person in the office opens the mail and separates the checks from the remittance advices. The checks are then endorsed with the company's "for deposit only" stamp and put in a file for deposit later in the day. The controller's clerk enters the customer's number and payment into the computer system using the information on the remittance advice. The cash receipt is entered into the system once the clerk has confirmed that the proper account and amount are displayed on the screen. The remittance advices are filed in the order they are processed; they are kept until the next working day and then destroyed. At 2:00 p.m., a two-part deposit slip is generated by the system.

- Copy 1 is taken to the bank in the afternoon (about 2:30 p.m.) along with the cash receipts from the file
- Copy 2 is filed by day in the controller's office

At the close of business hours (5:00 p.m.) each day, the computer information department prepares a backup tape of the current day's cash receipts activity. This backup tape is stored in a secure place in the event of a systems malfunction. After 10 working days, the tape is released for further use.

Cash and checks received from the accounts receivable billing department from over the counter sales are given to the person making the deposit that day and are included with the regular deposit, being noted as "cash sales."

Purchasing - Inventory Procedures

Raw materials are removed from the storeroom only on written or oral authorization of one of the production foremen. The raw materials warehouse clerk then records the raw materials as placed into the production process.

At the end of each day, the raw materials warehouse clerk checks the computer system to determine which items must be ordered. The system then generates requisitions for these items. The requisitions are sent to the purchasing department. The purchasing clerk then enters the appropriate data into the computer system to prepare a three-part purchase order. The complete purchase order is signed by the production manager who sends it to the purchasing agent, Stephanie Steale, for final approval.

- Copy 1 is sent to the vendor
- Copy 2 is filed in the purchasing department until the goods are received. It then becomes part of the cash disbursements records
- Copy 3 is filed by vendor in the purchasing department's history file

When the raw materials are received, a receiving clerk prepares a two-part serially numbered receiving report, which shows vendor, the items and the amounts received.

- Copy 1 is sent to the warehouse clerk with the inventory
- Copy 2 is filed in the receiving department by number

The warehouse clerk verifies the receiving clerk's count and reconciles any differences. The clerk then updates the perpetual inventory records on the warehouse computer by entering the amount received and the receiving report number. Any differences between the quantity received and the quantity ordered are listed on a printout. The printout is sent to the purchasing agent who reconciles any differences by communicating with the vendor. All of the day's receiving reports are then forwarded to the purchasing agent. The purchasing agent matches the receiving report with Copy 2 of the purchase order.

Vendor invoices are sent to the purchasing agent who matches them with the receiving reports and purchase orders. The three documents are sent to the accounts payable department to be entered into the computer system so that a voucher can be prepared. The information entered by the clerk updates the voucher register and accounts payable subsidiary and control ledgers. Each day the complete voucher packages (invoices, receiving reports, and purchase orders) are sent to the controller for approval. The voucher packages are then returned to the accounts payable department where they are filed in the unpaid bills file by due date.

Each day the system prints a list of vouchers requiring payment on that day. The clerk removes the voucher packages from the file and sends them to the cashier, Pennie Monie. The cashier then authorizes the system to print the checks. The cashier forwards the checks and the supporting voucher packages to the purchase agent who also approves the payment and enters information into the system to update the cash disbursements journal. The checks and supporting voucher packages are then forwarded to the controller who reviews the documentation and then signs the checks. All the documents are then sent to the treasurer who countersigns all checks over $50,000. The treasury clerk then marks the documents "paid" and sends the package to the mailroom clerk, Bob Boared, who mails the checks to the vendors and files the canceled voucher packages.

Inventory - Finished Goods Procedures

Finished goods coming off the production line are packaged and prepared for delivery to the appropriate warehouse and distribution facility. At the end of the day, the production clerk enters the daily production information and authorizes the system to print a three-part shipping order.

- Copy 1 is sent to the warehouse facility
- Copy 2 stays with the inventory and is given to the driver
- Copy 3 is filed in the production office by day

The finished inventory is shipped each morning by company trucks to the distribution facility. When the inventory is received by the distribution facility, a receiving clerk prepares a two-part serially numbered receiving report, which shows the items and amounts received.

- Copy 1 is sent to the finished goods warehouse clerk
- Copy 2 is filed in the receiving department by number

The finished goods warehouse clerk then matches the Copy 1 of the receiving report with the Copy 1 of the shipping order. Any differences are reconciled. The clerk then updates the perpetual inventory records on the warehouse computer by entering the amounts received and the receiving report numbers.

Proli Footwear
Internal Control Weaknesses Worksheet
December 31, 2014

General Financial Reporting

1. The billing clerk should not have access to journals and ledgers. Different employees should handle these functions.

Proli Footwear
Vertical Analysis ($ in 1,000)
December 31, 2014

	Balance	Common Size	Industry	Auditor Summary: Exceeds, below, equal to industry
Cash and Cash Equivalents	319	0.3%	5.2%	A
Trade Accounts Receivable, net	25,466	23.7%	19.8%	A
Inventories	43,668	40.7%	46.1%	A
Other Current Assets	4,718	4.4%	2.3%	A
Total Current Assets	74,171	69.1%	73.4%	A
Total Plant Assets	15,381	14.3%	16.1%	A
Total Intangible Assets	14,567	13.6%	2.4%	A
Other Assets	3,284	3.1%	8.1%	A
Total Assets	107,403	100.0%	100.0%	
Current Maturities of Long-Term Liabilities	441	0.4%	3.1%	A
Notes Payable	12,800	11.9%	16.6%	A
Accounts Payable and Accrued Expenses	11,735	10.9%	10.3%	A
Total Current Liabilities	24,976	23.3%	38.3%	A
Long Term Debt and Lease Obligations	5,962	5.6%	10.7%	A
Other Long-Term Liabilities	3,357	3.1%	4.1%	A
Total Liabilities	34,295	31.9%	53.1%	
Common Stock	50	0.0%		
Additional Paid in Capital	22,500	20.9%		
Retained Earnings	50,558	47.1%		
Total Stockholders' Equity	73,108	68.1%	46.9%	
Total Liabilities and Stockholders' Equity	107,403	100.0%	100.0%	

Auditor Overall Conclusion:

A = Agreed information to reference book containing industry statistics

Proli Footwear
Vertical Analysis ($ in 1,000)
December 31, 2014

	Balance	Common Size	Industry	Auditor Summary: Exceeds, below, equal to industry
Net Sales	146,745	100.0%	100.0%	
Cost of Goods Sold	108,712	74.1%	66.9%	A
Gross Profit	38,033	25.9%	33.1%	A
Selling and Administrative Expenses	32,876	22.4%	29.2%	A
Operating Income	5,157	3.5%	3.9%	A
Other Income/(Expense)	(1,465)	(1.0%)	1.3%	A
Income before Income Taxes	3,692	2.5%	2.6%	A
Income Tax Expense	1,600	1.1%		
Net Income	2,092	1.4%		

Auditor Overall Conclusion:

A = Agreed information to reference book containing industry statistics

Proli Footwear
Analytical Review Worksheet - Selected Ratios   (All amounts are in $1,000s)
December 31, 2014

	Industry Ratio	2014 Unaudited Amount	2014 Unaudited Ratio	2013 Unaudited Amount	2013 Unaudited Ratio	2012 Unaudited Amount	2012 Unaudited Ratio
PROFITABILITY RATIOS							
Gross Profit Margin:	33.1% A						
Gross Profit ÷				44,892		37,203	
Net Sales				160,053	28.0%	134,197	27.7%
Return On Sales	4.5% A						
Net Income ÷				7,457		5,925	
Net Sales				160,053	4.7%	134,197	4.4%
Return on Equity:	16.2% A						
Net Income ÷				7,457		5,925	
Equity (Ending)				68,620	10.9%	62,576	9.5%
Return on Total Assets:	9.6% A						
Net Income ÷				7,457		5,925	
Total Assets(Ending)				112,113	6.7%	101,516	5.8%

Profitability appears to be [increasing decreasing, unchanged, not relevant].
Discuss income trend and the effect on the return ratios.
How does Proli compare to the industry?

Auditor summary of profitability: Are there any specific accounts that should be tested more thoroughly than others?

	Industry Ratio	2014 Unaudited Amount	2014 Unaudited Ratio	2013 Unaudited Amount	2013 Unaudited Ratio	2012 Unaudited Amount	2012 Unaudited Ratio
SOLVENCY RATIO							
Debt to equity:	72.0% A						
Total Liabilities ÷				43,493		38,940	
Total Equity(Ending)				68,620	63.4%	62,576	62.2%

Solvency is [improving, worse, no change, not relevant].
How does Proli compare to the industry?

Auditor summary of solvency: Are there any specific accounts that should be tested more thoroughly than others?

Proli Footwear
Analytical Review Worksheet - Selected Ratios   (All amounts are in 1,000s)
December 31, 2014

	Industry Ratio	2014 Unaudited Amount	2014 Unaudited Ratio	2013 Unaudited Amount	2013 Unaudited Ratio	2012 Unaudited Amount	2012 Unaudited Ratio
LIQUIDITY RATIOS							
Current Ratio:	3.4 A						
Current Assets ÷				78,715		69,286	
Current Liabilities				24,874	3.2	16,747	4.1
Quick Ratio:	1.4 A						
Cash + Acc Receivable (net) ÷				30,598		30,164	
Current Liabilities				24,874	1.2	16,747	1.8
TURNOVER							
Accts Receivable Turnover:	9.4 A						
Net Sales ÷				160,053		134,197	
Average Acc Receivable				26,453	6.1	24,297	5.5
Average Accts Receivable (Net)							
Acc Receivalbe-Beginning				22,776		25,817	
+ Acc Receivable-Ending				30,129		22,776	
Average (sum÷2)					26,453		24,297
Inventory Turnover:	4.1 A						
Cost of Sales ÷				115,161		96,994	
Average Inventory				38,842	3.0	33,256	2.9
Average Inventory:							
Inventory-Beginning				34,704		31,807	
+ Inventory-Ending				42,980		34,704	
Average (sum÷2)					38,842		33,256

Liquidity rates are [improving, worsening, unchanged, not relevant].

The accounts receivable turnover trend is [favorable, unfavorable]. Explain.

The inventory turnover trend is [favorable, unfavorable]. Explain.

How does Proli compare to the industry?

Auditor summary of liquidity: Are there any specific accounts that should be tested more thoroughly than others?

AUDITOR OVERALL CONCLUSION: Based on this analysis, which areas deserve greater audit emphasis?

A = Agreed information to reference book containing industry statistics

*Note: 2009 balances are not available so end-of-year amounts rather than averages are used to calculate ratios. RP

Proli Footwear
Assessment of Risk of Material Errors and Irregularities Worksheet
December 31, 2014

Factor	Lower Risk	Higher Risk	Auditor Comment	Auditor Risk Assessment: 1=low, 2=moderate, 3=high
Management Characteristics:				
Management turnover	Low	High	*3 key middle managers hired by competition in 2012*	
Emphasis on meeting earnings projections	Little	Very high	*in process of preparing budget and profit planning systems*	
Reputation in business community	Honest	Improper conduct	*active and well respected in CT*	
Management attitude on financial reporting	Complies with GAAP	Looks for loopholes	*just hired new VP-finance-prior VP not CMA or CPA*	
Management operating style	Effective oversight group	Domination by single person	*strong family influence*	
Auditor Assessment of Management Characteristics = Sum of Above				
Operating Characteristics:				
Status of industry	Healthy / Mixed / Distressed		*healthy*	
Profitability relative to the industry	Adequate	Inadequate	*somewhat lower than industry*	
Sensitivity of operating results to economy	Low	Very sensitive	*inelastic demand*	
Organizational structure	Centralized	Decentralized with inadequate monitoring	*centralized*	
Rate of change in industry	Slow	Rapid	*customer & marketing driven*	
Indications of going concern problems	None	Substantial doubt	*none*	
Auditor Assessment of Operating Characteristics = Sum of Above				
Engagement Characteristics:				
Misstatements in prior audits	Few	Many	*no prior audits*	
Difficult to audit transactions	Few	Many	*leases*	
Relationship with client	Repeat engagement	First audit	*first audit*	
Related party transactions	None	Any	*unknown-but not anticipated*	
Difficult accounting issues	Few	Many	*not many anticipated*	
Auditor Assessment of Engagement Characteristics = Sum of Above				
OVERALL RISK ASSESSMENT = Sum of Three Sections				
Overall Risk Assessment Ratings: 16-25 = Low		26-35 = Moderate		36-49 = High

Proli Footwear
Analysis of Audit Risk Worksheet
December 31, 2014

Audit Section	Audit Risk	Inherent Risk	Control Risk*	Targeted Detection Risk	Indicate level of evidence required (Low, Moderate, High, Very High)	Indicate primary timing of audit tests (Interim or Year-End)	Ranking for amount of audit evidence required (1=lowest; 7=highest)
Cash	10%	20%	70%				
Accounts Receivable and Sales	1%	25%	20%				
Inventory and Accounts Payable	1%	50%	50%				
Long-Lived Assets	3%	25%	20%				
Current Liabilities	1%	50%	80%				
Non Current Liabilities	1%	40%	50%				
Equities	5%	20%	20%				

Auditor Conclusions:

In which audit section does the **greatest** amount of audit resources need to be allocated?

In which audit section does the **least** amount of audit resources need to be allocated?

* Control risk is based on the preliminary assessment of internal control

NOTE: $DR = AR/(IR * CR)$

Proli Footwear
Planning Materiality Worksheet
December 31, 2014

A. Planning Materiality = auditor's preliminary judgment about materiality levels; used as a guide to determine whether audit adjustments should be recognized

Gross revenue _____

Total assets _____

Base Amount (larger of total revenue or total assets): _____

Planning materiality calculation*:

Amount from table	Percentage from table	Base Amount	Planning Materiality

---

B. Tolerable Misstatement = amount by which a specific account can be misstated without causing financial statements to be materially misleading

Planning Materiality	Commonly used factor 0.70	Tolerable Misstatement

---

C. Testing Threshold = Materiality Threshold = value that, if exceeded, warrants specific level of investigation

	Tolerable Misstatement	Testing Threshold**

---

* West and Fair, CPAs, LLC uses the following table as a guideline when calculating planning materiality.

If the Base Amount is:		Planning Materiality is:
Over	But not over	Amount + (Percent x Base)
$0	$ 5 million	9,000 + 1.0%
$ 5 million	$10 million	30,000 + 0.5%
$ 50 million		150,000 + 0.25%

** West & Fair, CPAs, LLC uses 1/3 of the tolerable misstatement

AUDIT MEMO
West & Fair CPAs, LLC
Stamford, CT

Re: Proli Footwear
"Brainstorming Session"
December 18, 2014

The following members took part in a brainstorming session to discuss the potential for material misstatements due to fraud: Patricia Fair, Richard West, and RP.
The following items were discussed and considered:
Events or conditions that indicate incentives/pressures to misstate financial statements:
- Sales and profitability declined in 2014
- Negative operating CF in 2014
- Slow inventory and A/R turnover compared to industry
- Middle market company
- Management talking to underwriters
  - IPO planned within 3-5 years
- Family owned business

Opportunities to misstate financial statements:
- Strong family influence, especially Chairman of the Board, Samuel Sole, Jr.
- Board of Directors not actively involved in governance
- Audit Committee just formed to meet current requirements for publicly traded companies
  - Controller is member of Audit Committee
- Middle manager turnover to competition
- Appear to be no complex transactions
- Manual accounting system – many approvals required
- 3 operating locations – small centralized management and accounting functions
- Simple lines of command
- Long-standing employees
- No internal audit function
- Don't anticipate any related party transactions
- Management does not understand information technology
  - Company is behind the curve in computerizing operations
  - Company systems are not integrated

Attitudes/rationalizations to justify to misstating financial statements:
- No previous audits
- No code of ethics

The following accounts may be susceptible to material misstatement:
- Revenue
- Inventory
- Accounts Receivable
- Accounts Payable

Planning Memo

The Senior in charge of this audit has partially drafted the planning memo for this year's audit. You have been asked to complete this memo.

AUDIT MEMO
West & Fair CPAs, LLC
Stamford, CT

Re: Proli Footwear
Planning Memo
December 31, 2014

In planning the audit engagement for Proli Footwear for the year ended December 31, 2014, the following matters have been considered.

1. The objective of this engagement is _____ on the financial statements.

2. This is the first time the Company has been audited. In preparation for the 2014 audit, we observed the 2013 physical inventory count and tested the purchase and sales cut-offs.

3. The company has assets of approximately $ _____ and total revenue of approximately $_____. These amounts are expected to change as we propose adjustments for accruals and so on.

4. The internal control is deemed [poor / fair / good / excellent] for a medium-sized manufacturing firm. Management's attitude toward internal control is _____

_____

5. Proli is a closely held family owned Company. The Company plans on going public within the next five years.

6. The Company follows generally accepted accounting principles. The prior chief financial officer did not keep up with GAAP and made occasional errors. The Company relies on our firm to provide the proper application of GAAP.

7. Materiality was calculated to be _____. Since the president wants our firm to ensure that items are recorded to close tolerances, we will propose and record all adjustments we find, even if the adjustments in the aggregate are less than the materiality level.

8. The testing threshold for individually significant items is $ _____.

9. Based on a preliminary assessment of the Company's operating procedures, we can expect the more material adjustments affecting income to occur in the following areas_____

_____

10. I expect that our firm will be able to render _____ opinion. However, this expectation may change as the audit progresses.

Proli Footwear
Time Control
December 31, 2014

Section	Budgeted Time	Time Spent Working with Team	Time Spent Working Alone
2. Planning the Audit	5 hours		

Team member names:

ASSIGNMENT #3 – CASH

ASSIGNMENT

1. Complete each step of the cash audit program. Indicate completion for each step by making sure that the step is initialed, dated, and that the workpaper reference is indicated. For those audit program steps that are already initialed as having been completed, enter an appropriate date and workpaper reference next to the initials.

2. Be sure to use the appropriate tickmarks to indicate the specific work performed on each piece of audit documentation.

3. Complete and submit for grading all the audit documentation for this section organized in the following sequence:
   a. Audit program with dates, initials and audit documentation references;
   b. Completed Lead Schedule with workpaper references, tickmarks indicating work done and appropriate sign-offs;
   c. Specific audit workpaper schedules in sequence with workpaper references, as appropriate, tickmarks indicating work done and appropriate sign-offs;
   d. Adjusting Journal Entry Contol containing the proposed AJEs;
   e. Red Flag Events;
   f. Management Letter Comments containing recommended improvements to internal control and other operating issues;
   g. Updated Time Control Worksheet; and
   h. Updated Working Trial Balance (WTB).

4. Each adjusting entry should be entered on the following audit documentation:
   a. Appropriate workpaper schedule
   b. Lead schedule
   c. AJE control
   d. Working trial balance

AUDIT PROGRAM – CASH

Procedures	Initials	Date	W/P Ref
General			
1. Foot and crossfoot lead schedule and all other PBC schedules, e.g., bank reconciliation.			
2. Compare balances on other PBC schedules with balances on lead schedules			
3. Compare balances on lead schedules with account balances in the trial balance			
Analytical Review Procedures			
1. Review entries to general ledger cash accounts and investigate unusual (including General Journal) entries to Petty Cash, Cash in Bank-Operating, and Cash in Bank-Payroll accounts	RP		
2. Review monthly bank reconciliations of Cash in Bank-Operating and Cash in Bank-Payroll accounts.	RP		

Procedures	Initials	Date	W/P Ref
Substantive Procedures - *Petty Cash*			
1. Count petty cash and have petty cash custodian sign audit documentation at conclusion of count.	RP		
2. Complete petty cash audit documentation and prepare adjusting entry, if necessary.			
Cash in Bank - Operating and Payroll			
3. Obtain bank confirmations at year-end and cutoff bank statements as of January 8, 2014.	RP		
4. Compare items on bank cutoff statements to cash receipts and the check register, noting differences.			
5. Complete interbank cash transfer analysis for December. Verify proper recording of interbank transfers			
Cash in Bank - Operating			
6. Verify correctness of bank reconciliation by:			
a. Tracing the deposit(s) to the cash receipts journal and the bank cutoff statement.			
b. Comparing outstanding checks with entries in the check register and with the information included on the bank cutoff statement.			
c. Preparing adjusting entry, if necessary.			
7. Verify clerical accuracy of selected payrolls:			
a. Several during the year	RP		
b. December 31, 2014	RP		
8. Verify accuracy of payroll deductions with personnel records.	RP		
9. Trace net payroll to check register:			
a. Several during the year	RP		
b. December 31, 2014	RP		
Cash in Bank - Payroll			
10. Verify correctness of bank reconciliation by:			
a. Tracing deposits in transit, if any, to the check register and to the bank cutoff statement	RP		
b. Comparing December 31 net payroll to charges on the payroll bank account cut off statement to determine that all payroll checks cleared the bank.	RP		
c. Preparing adjusting entry, if necessary	RP		
Cash-All Accounts			
11. Review for proper financial statement disclosure and classification, noting restrictions on cash, if any.	RP		

HELPFUL HINTS FROM THE IN-CHARGE ACCOUNTANT:

1. Use a tickmark to show each work procedure performed.

2. Be alert for "Red Flag" events. A red flag event is an event or transaction that might indicate fraudulent activity, but needs further investigation to determine:
   a. Whether it was intentional or just human error and
   b. The impact of the event.

3. Refer to an accounting text and read about the nature of an imprest fund and how it might affect the operation of the payroll bank account and the petty cash fund. Also determine how reporting on the financial statements could be affected by the use of an imprest fund.

4. Be aware of the cutoff dates for cash receipts and disbursements.

5. Remember that any work RP has completed need not be repeated by you. You may assume that RP has done all the necessary work to complete the work program step correctly. *All of RP's work looks like this.*

Proli Footwear
Lead Schedule - Cash
December 31, 2014

Account Number	Account Title	Balance per T/B Debit	Balance per T/B Credit	- - - Adjustments - - - Debit	Credit	Balance per Audit Debit	Credit
1000	Imprest Petty Cash Fund	3,000					
1010	Cash - Operating	166,083					
1020	Imprest Payroll Cash Account	0					
1030	Cash - Money Market Account	150,000 ×					
	Total	319,083					

Impact of AJEs for this assignment on net income before income taxes = _____ DR/CR

× = Interest Income of $4,700 included in Misc Non-Operating Income (Account #8500) – Not material for reclassification   RP

40

Proli Footwear
Imprest Petty Cash Fund Reconciliation
December 31, 2014

Counted on December 30, 2014 in the presence of Brian Baddude, petty cash custodian			
Bills		$535.00	
Coins		8.31	
Stamps		6.44	
Total currency and stamps			549.75 f
Vouchers:			
Emergency travel advance - V Vamp	b)	$1,200.00	∟
Emergency travel advance - G Buye	b)	800.00	∟
Postage stamps	a)	99.00	
Supplies for office	a)	26.00	
COD receipt for supplies	a)	32.00	
Cash advance - Brian Baddude	b)	50.00	∟
Gas receipt - John Jones travel	c)	42.00	
V Vamp - Lunch with visitors	c)	157.00	∟
Total vouchers			2,406.00 f
Petty cash fund total			2,955.75 f

Returned to me intact: *Brian Baddude*
Counted by: RP 12/30/14

Shortage/(overage)	d)	44.25	
Balance per trial balance		3,000.00 f	
Audit adjustments:			
Balance per audit			

f = footed

∟ = Lacks approval signature; Company policy requires approval of person other than person receiving the advance.

41

Proli Footwear
Bank Reconciliation - Operating Account
December 31, 2014

				Per Client	Correct
Balance per Bank - December 31, 2014				$491,224	
Deposits in transit per Cash Receipts Journal 12/31/2014				85,000	
Subtotal				576,224	
Outstanding checks:	Check #	Date	Amount		
ABC Leather (1)	2225	2/20/2012	15,074		
GGG Corp. (1)	2742	12/23/2012	975		
CT Telephone Co.	3706	12/15/2014	2,750		
Scuff GB Leather	3713	12/23/2014	132,575		
Waterbury Real Estate Taxes	3714	12/23/2014	23,500		
Bug Computers	3715	12/23/2014	128,750		
Red Cross/Shield	3717	12/28/2014	12,700		
City of Proli	3718	12/28/2014	12,500		
Potor Properties	3719	12/30/2014	8,017		
Elfriede's Famous Fabrics (2)	3720	12/30/2014	73,300		
Total Outstanding Checks				410,141	
Balance per trial balance				166,083	
Audit adjustments:					

Balance per audit

(1) These companies have ceased doing business. State law regarding outstanding checks does NOT apply to this situation. RP

(2) Bank cut-off statement shows this check is for $46,300. The difference of $27,000 was paid to and cashed by Western GB Leather in check #3721. The sum of the two checks equals the amount shown for Elfriede's Famous Fabrics of $73,300. RP

(3) Examined the December bank statement to determine whether any outstanding checks were not included in this reconciliation. On December 27, 2014 a wire transfer of $30,000 that was not recorded per books was made to Lucky Advertising. RP

(4) The president of Scuff GB leather is Joan Scuff, wife of Goodwin Buye. This requires further investigation for related party implications.

Proli Footwear
Interbank Cash Transfer Analysis
December 31, 2014

| From operating account: | | | To payroll account: | |
Date	Check #	Amount	Date	Amount
12/04/2014	3584	48,640	12/05/2014	48,640
12/18/2014	3705	48,000	12/19/2014	48,000
01/02/2015	3724			

Proli Footwear
Partial Bank Cutoff Statements
December 31, 2014

Operating Account

Date	Check #	Amount	Deposits	Deposits	Balance
12/31/2014					461,224
1/2/2015	3724	148,600 (1)	52,500		365,124
1/5/2015	3713	132,575	408,175	28,900	669,624
1/6/2015	3715	128,750	315,763		856,637
1/7/2015	3720	46,300	140,595		950,932
1/7/2015	3721	27,000			923,932
	3714	23,500			900,432
1/8/2015	3718	12,500	217,655		1,105,587
	3722	8,250			1,097,337
	3723	23,000			1,074,337
	3725	124,380			949,957
	3727	23,500			926,457
	3717	12,700			913,757
	3719	8,017			905,740

Payroll Account

Date	Check #	Amount	Deposits	Balance
12/31/2014				0
1/2/2015	5105	2,666	148,600 (1)	145,934
	5124	615		145,319
	5116	462		144,857
	5112	462		144,395
	5101	5,000		139,395
	5107	770		138,625
	5122	615		138,010
	5109	615		137,395
	5102	4,000		133,395
	5106	770		132,625

(1) See Schedule EA-2. RP. Employee payroll checks were distributed on 12/31/14 in payment of December accrual. The book entry recorded in the general ledger on 12/31/14 was:

Salary expense	48,600	
Bonus expense	100,000	EA-6
Accrued expenses		148,600

Proli Footwear
Excerpts from Cash Receipts Journal

Date	Customer	Amount		Total Deposit
12/28/2014	AAA Shoes	64,325		
	Barb's Boots	51,866		
	Cash Sales	1,895		118,086
12/29/2014	Sam's Sabot Sellers	345,000		
	Mary's Mocs	125,789		470,789
12/31/2014	Allen Shoe Store	9,526	1)	T
	Happy Feet	13,566		T
	Conn Shoe Seller	17,134		T
	Walking Feet	15,874		T
	Leather Scrap Inc-cash sale	28,900	2)	85,000
1/5/2015	Harmony Shoe Co	301,575		
	Shoe Mart	61,600		
	Proli Shoe Outlet	45,000		408,175
1/6/2015	Alpha Best Shoes	128,900		
	Well Heeled Footwear	186,863		315,763
1/7/2015	Ollie's Oxfords	51,500		
	Boots by Bob	59,095		110,595
1/8/2015	Easy Comfort Shoes	28,900		
	Sal's Soles	166,750		
	Footcare Inc.	11,500		
	Sizes for All	10,505		217,655
1/9/2015	Fashion Hound	104,411		
	Conn Shoe Seller	2,584		
	Betty's Booties	11,874		118,869

1) Per deposit ticket copy, amount listed is $5,926; client states that $5,926 is amount of invoice RP

2) Per client, sale occurred and payment received on 1/2/15 and the deposit was made on 1/5/15. RP

T = Traced to copy of deposit receipt noting that deposit date is 1/2/15

Proli Footwear
Excerpts from Operating Account Check Register (1/2)

Date	Check #	Payee		Amount
12/18/2014	3705	Payroll Transfer		48,000
	3706	CT Telephone Co		2,750
	3707	Performance Truck Repair		8,590
	3708	Walton Trust		354,302
	3709	Lucky Advertising		58,000
	3710	Petty Cash Custodian		1,300
	3711	Proli Florist		125
	3712	Computer Supply House		9,750
12/23/2014	3713	Scuff GB Leather	a)	132,575
	3714	Waterbury real estate taxes		23,500
	3715	Bug Computers		128,750
12/26/2014	3716	City of Proli-personal property taxes		10,646
	3717	Red Cross/Shield		12,700
	3718	City of Proli-real estate taxes		12,500
12/30/2014	3719	Waterbury personal property taxes		8,017
	3720	Elfriede's Famous Fabrics	1)	73,300
	3721	Void **	2)	
1/2/2015	3722	Fred's Cleaning Service		8,250
	3723	Standard Adhesive		23,000
	3724	Payroll Transfer		148,600
	3725	Big City Office Supply		124,380
	3726	Blue Star Restaurant		1,175
	3727	Connecticut Electric Co		23,500
	3728	Thumpen, Lumpem & Howe, Attorneys		130,000
	3729	Potor Trash Removal		23,000
	3730	Carlisle Chemicals		90,994
1/5/2015	3731	Proli Accounting Temps		35,800
	3732	Lincoln Leather		58,900
	3733	Veritech Adhesives		32,842
	3734	P&P Mobile Phone		25,600
	3735	Vijay Vinyl Supply		85,900
	3736	Lucky Leathers		12,500
	3737	Lucky Advertising		57,000

1) See A-5 cutoff statement; amount of this check should be $46,300   RP

2) See A-5 cutoff statement; this check was not voided; cancelled check shows this was paid to Scuff GB Leather** for $27,000.   RP

a) Scuff GB Leather is owned by Joan Scuff, wife of Goodwin Buye. Is there a related party issue?   RP

Proli Footwear
Excerpts from Operating Account Check Register (2/2)

Date	Check #	Payee	Amount
1/5/2015	3738	Scuff GB Leather**	86,935
	3739	Connecticut Propane	27,600
	3740	Waterbury Trash Service	7,890
1/6/2015	3741	Lucky Advertising	300,000
	3742	Connecticut Phone	192,150
	3743	Connecticut Phone	187,680
1/7/2015	3744	Proli Florist	27,890
	3745	Waterbury Gas	38,950
	3746	Local National Bank	23,408
1/9/2015	3747	Local National Bank	10,646
	3748	Workers' Comp Insurance Agency	731,500
1/10/2015	3749	Walton Trust	6,238
	3750	Walton Electric	78,800
	3751	Proli Propane	66,600
	3752	Florida Phone	144,400
1/12/2015	3753	Walton Trust	11,402
	3754	Waterbury Water	141,580
	3755	Proli Water	136,780
	3756	Connecticut Electric	75,450
	3757	Proli Insurance Agency	788,900
	3758	Walton Water	158,420
1/14/2015	3759	Payroll Transfer	61,000
	3760	Proli Stock Agent: Dec dividend	500,000
	3761	Proli Electric	63,800
	3762	Walton Gas Company	58,700
	3763	Walton Mobile Phones	22,750
	3764	Proli Rental Properties, LLC (L1, L2A, L2B)	37,258
	3765	Alice Fair Real Estate Associates (L4, L5) 1)	21,387
	3766	Walton Properties (L3)	4,540
	3767	Nebraska Leather	25,000

1) Alice Fair was married to Patricia Fair's brother, Frank Fair, until their divorce in 2008. Does this affect auditor independence? RP

PROLI FOOTWEAR
STAMFORD, CONNECTICUT

January 5, 2015

Proli National Bank
Proli, CT

Dear Sirs:

Our independent auditors, West & Fair CPAs, LLC, are performing an audit of our financial statements. We have provided our accountants with information regarding deposit and loan balances as of *December 31, 2014*. Please confirm the accuracy of this information, noting any discrepancies in the information provided. If other balances are outstanding, please include that information. Please return this letter directly to our accountants: *West & Fair CPAs, LLC; Stamford, CT*

1. Deposit information

Account Name	Account No.	Interest Rate	Balance	
Checking	95870	None	$461,224	
Payroll	95872	None	$ 0	
Money Market	55877	4.2%	$150,000	(interest has been paid through 12/31/14)

2. Loan information

Account No. Description	Balance	Date Due	Interest Rate	Date through Which Interest Is Paid	Description of Collateral
None					

Very truly yours,

Harold F. Heele,

Harold F. Heele,
Vice President – Finance and Chief Financial Officer

CONFIRMATION: The information presented above is in agreement with our records. Although we have not performed a detailed search of our records, no other deposit or loan accounts have come to our attention except as noted below.

Exceptions or Comments: *NONE*

Joan Bankeret	_January 12, 2015_	_Assistant Bank Manager_
(Institution's Authorized Signature)	(Date)	(Title)

Proli Footwear
AJE Control - Cash
December 31, 2014

AJE Number	Reference	Accounts/Description	Account Number	Debit	Credit

x = account has impact on income before taxes amount
Impact on income before taxes =   DR/CR

Proli Footwear
Red Flag Events - Cash
December 31, 2014

Event Number	Reference	Auditor Observation

Proli Footwear
Management Letter Comments - Cash
December 31, 2014

Comment Number	Reference	Auditor Observation/ Recommendation	Benefit to Client
1	A-2	Control over petty cash fund appears to be poor. Need to put petty cash procedures in writing. The custodian and officer took advances with no documentation.	Better control over petty cash.

Proli Footwear
Time Control
December 31, 2014

Section	Budgeted Time	Time Spent Working with Team	Time Spent Working Alone
3. Cash	6 hours		

Team member names:

ASSIGNMENT #4 – ACCOUNTS RECEIVABLE AND SALES

ASSIGNMENT

1. Complete each step of the accounts receivable and sales audit program. Indicate completion for each step by making sure that the step is initialed, dated, and that the workpaper reference is indicated. For those audit program steps that are already initialed as having been completed, enter an appropriate date and workpaper reference next to the initials.

2. Be sure to use the appropriate tickmarks to indicate the specific work performed on each piece of audit documentation.

3. Complete and submit for grading all the audit documentation for this section organized in the following sequence:
   a. Audit program with dates, initials and audit documentation references;
   b. Completed Lead Schedule with workpaper references, tickmarks indicating work done and appropriate sign-offs;
   c. Specific audit workpaper schedules in sequence with workpaper references, as appropriate, tickmarks indicating work done and appropriate sign-offs;
   d. Adjusting Journal Entry Control containing the proposed AJEs;
   e. Red Flag Events;
   f. Management Letter Comments containing recommended improvements to internal control and other operating issues;
   g. Updated Time Control Worksheet; and
   h. Updated Working Trial Balance (WTB).

4. Each adjusting entry should be entered on the following audit documentation:
   a. Appropriate workpaper schedule
   b. Lead schedule
   c. AJE control
   d. Working trial balance

AUDIT PROGRAM – ACCOUNTS RECEIVABLE AND SALES

Procedures	Initials	Date	W/P Ref
General			
1. Foot and crossfoot lead schedule and all other PBC schedules.			
2. Compare balances on lead schedules with account balances in the trial balance.			
3. Compare balances on other PBC schedules with balances			

Procedures	Initials	Date	W/P Ref

Analytical Review Procedures

1. Note any unusual relationships between current and prior year balances including the following: gross sales, returns and allowances, and discounts, receivables, allowance account, and bad debts expense.

    RP 2/15

2. Scan for unusual entries to above accounts. Analyze entries from general journal to these accounts.

    RP 2/15 B-7

Substantive Procedures

1. Perform sales cutoff procedures to determine that sales and receivables are recorded in the proper period:

    a. Examine sales invoices shown on the cut-off analysis for clerical accuracy, proper pricing, and completeness.

       RP

    b. Compare cut-off analysis with shipping records.

       RP

    c. Review credit memos issued after year-end for authorization

       RP

    d. Determine that sales and returns are posted in the proper accounting period

2. Obtain the aged accounts receivable analysis.

    a. On a test basis, trace:

       i. Selected customer account balances to aging schedule

          RP

       ii. Selected account balances on aging schedule to subsidiary ledger

          RP

       iii. Selected invoices to customer accounts

          RP

       iv. Selected cash receipts to customer account

          RP

3. Determine number of customer accounts to be confirmed.

    RP 1/8/15

    a. Send confirmations to selected accounts.

       RP

    b. Prepare a summary of confirmation replies.

       RP

    c. Review the replies on the confirmation summary schedule and prepare any necessary adjusting entries.

4. Analyze the allowance for doubtful accounts and complete the appropriate audit documentation. Prepare an entry to adjust the bad debt expense and allowance accounts.

HELPFUL HINTS FROM THE IN-CHARGE ACCOUNTANT:

1. Use a tickmark to show each work procedure performed.

2. Remember to post adjusting entries affecting the accounts receivable and sales section from the cash section to the accounts receivable lead sheet.

3. Be alert for "Red Flag" events. A red flag event is an event or transaction that might indicate fraudulent activity, but needs further investigation to determine:
   a. Whether it was intentional or just human error and
   b. The impact of the event.

4. FOB refers to the point at which the title for goods being sold transfers from Proli to the customer.

5. Proli uses the delivery expense account as a clearing account for payments to freight carriers and reimbursements from customers.

6. If you think inventory needs to be adjusted, include that information on the TO DO list for the person working on the inventory assignment. (i.e. all inventory adjustments will be made in the inventory assignment #5).

7. When completing the allowance for doubtful accounts worksheet, remember to update the Accounts Receivable balance for all adjusting entries made in this assignment.

8. Remember that any work RP has completed need not be repeated by you. You may assume that RP has done all the necessary work to complete the work program step correctly. *All of RP's work looks like this.*

Proli Footwear
Lead Schedule - Accounts Receivable and Sales
December 31, 2014

Account Number	Account Title	Balance per T/B		- - - - - Adjustments - - - - -		Balance per Audit	
		Debit	Credit	Debit	Credit	Debit	Credit
1200	Accounts Receivable	26,566,100					
1250	Allowance for Doubtful Accounts		1,100,000				
7100	Bad Debt Expense	880,000					
5000	Sales		148,235,225				
5100	Sales Discounts	372,191					
5200	Sales Returns & Allowances	1,117,535					
7150	Delivery Expense	2,504,230					

Impact of AJEs for this assignment on net income before income taxes=   DR/CR

56

Proli Footwear - Sales Cut-off Analysis - December 31, 2014

Customer	Account Number	Invoice Number	Cash #1010	Accounts Receivable #1200	Delivery Expense #7150	Sales #5000	Sales Returns #5200	Product Cost	Auditor Comments	Auditor Action
12/29/14 Hot Harvey Puppies	27137	V 8518		12,278	504	11,774		8,850	shipped FOB shipping point on 12/29/14	NONE
Athlete's Shoes	27100	V 8519		85,190	877	84,313		63,299	shipped FOB shipping point on 12/29/14	
12/30/14 Pat's Poulaines	27158	V 8520		25,106	148	24,958		17,177	shipped FOB shipping point on 12/29/14	
Dickies' Dogs	27121	V 8521		(8,076)	(101)		(7,975)	5,781	credit memo sent to customer	
12/31/14 Boots by Bob	27119	V 8522		17,856	389	17,467		12,576	shipped FOB customer's San Diego Warehouse on 12/31/14	
Miracle Heel	27153	V 8523		38,901	419	38,482		28,861	shipped FOB shipping point on 12/31/14	
Leather Scrap Inc		V 8524	28,900			28,900			See A-6	Adjustment made on A-6
1/4/15 Terra Shoes	27178	V 8525		43,910	800	43,110		33,625	shipped FOB shipping point on 1/4/15	
Biker's Best	27117	V 8526		54,901	866	54,035		42,650	shipped FOB shipping point on 12/30/14	
1/5/15 Ollie's Oxfords	27156	V 8527		71,370	1,400	69,970		51,070	shipped FOB shipping point on 1/5/15	
Easy Comfort Shoes	27129	V 8528		55,555	1,035	54,520		40,350	shipped FOB shipping point on 1/5/15	
1/6/15 Footwear Wearhouse	27135	E 8529		(22,581)			(22,581)	17,380	Customer returned overstock; received by Proli on 12/29/14	
Running Shoes, Inc	27160	V 8530		118,455	1,508	116,947		88,880	shipped FOB shipping point on 1/6/15	

V = vouched to invoice copy and shipping records   RP   E = examined credit memo copy and receiving report. RP

Proli Footwear - Accounts Receivable Aging and Summary - December 31, 2014

Name	Account #	Balance	Current	Over 30	Over 60	Over 90
Althlete's Shoes	27100 *C SL CF*	941,356 a	736,546	204,810		
Athletic Fit	27101 *C SL CF*	1,119,104 a	831,160	287,944		
Barb's Boots	27115 *C SL CF*	583,128 a			583,128	
Big Toe Fashions	27116 *C SL CF*	22,345 b				22,345
Biker's Best	27117 *C SL CF*	460,837 a	358,740		102,097	
Bonnie's Balmorals	27118 *C SL CF*	864,088 a	864,088			
Boots by Bob	27119 *C SL CF*	532,841 a	189,000	343,841		
Charlene's Chopines	27120 *C SL CF*	648,804 a	623,828		24,976	
Dickie's Dogs	27121 *C SL CF*	-248,788 c	-248,788			
Easy Comfort Shoes	27129 *C SL CF*	1,194,801 a	1,194,801			
Fashion Hound	27133 *C SL CF*	104,411 b				104,411
Footcare Inc.	27134 *C SL CF*	991,723 a	98,680	293,506	599,537	
Harmony Shoe	27136 *C SL CF*	301,575 a	301,575			
Hot Harvey Puppies	27137 *C SL CF*	56,189 b				56,189
Leather by Last	27149 *C SL CF*	967,832 a	967,832			
Leather Footwear	27151 *C SL CF*	970,477 a	970,477			
Leather Leaders	27152 *C SL CF*	840,670 a		840,670		
Miracle Heel	27153 *C SL CF*	75,888 b				75,888
Moccasins by Maureen	27154 *C SL CF*	124,787 a		124,787		
Moccasins for All	27155 *C SL CF*	550,068 a		108,708	441,360	
Ollie's Oxfords	27156 *C SL CF*	739,582 a	739,582			
Pat's Poulaines	27158 *C SL CF*	118,650 b				118,650
Planet Venus Shoes	27159 *C SL CF*	4,766 b				4,766
Running Shoes, Inc.	27160 *C SL CF*	982,313 a	982,313			
Sal's Soles	27175 *C SL CF*	664,997 a	664,997			
Sam's Sabot Sellers	27176 *C SL CF*	943,613 a	943,613			
Shoes for All	27177 *C SL CF*	893,686 a	893,686			
Terra Shoes	27178 *C SL CF*	0				
Terta Shoes	27179 *C SL CF*	99,122 b				99,122
Toe Poppers	27180 *C SL CF*	37,188 b				37,188
Walking Well	27183 *C SL CF*	612,597 a	516,797	95,800		
Well Heeled Footwear	27184 *C SL CF*	997,305 a	97,100	900,205		
Other 145 confirmed accounts	*CF*	2,236,846	1,795,556	145,776	95,427	200,087
Other 1,359 accounts not confirmed	*CF*	7,133,299	2,413,048	4,216,793	503,458	
Totals - 1,536 accounts		26,566,100	15,934,631	7,562,840	2,349,983	718,646
		F	F	F	F	F

Note: All accounts shown were confirmed. See the confirmation summary worksheet for the results of this test.
RP SL = Traced account balance to accounts receivable subsidiary ledger   F = Footed   CF = Crossfooted
C = Confirmation sent to customer. Σa=16,926,184 B-4 ; Σb=518,559 B-4; Σc= 248,788 B-4;

58

Proli Footwear
Determination of Sample Size for Substantive Tests of Accounts Receivable
Using a Formal Nonstatistical Sampling Plan
December 31, 2014

		Number of Customers	Amount
Tolerable misstatement for each account balance:	II-6		364,412
Testing threshold: West & Fair, CPAs, LLC uses 1/3 of tolerable misstatement	II-6		121,471 b)
Accounts Receivable Balance:	B-3	1,536	26,566,100
Accounts exceeding threshold:	B-3 (Σa)	22	16,926,184
Unusual items:			
Very delinquent balances (over 90 days)	B-3 (Σb)	8	518,559
Large credit balances	B-3 (Σc)	1	(248,788)
Large sales recorded just prior to year-end		0	0
Untested amount		1,505	8,872,569 a)
Additional accounts to be tested	e)	146	2,236,846
Total accounts to be tested		177	19,432,801

It has been determined that a moderate level of reliance can be placed on other audit procedures for accounts receivable/sales cycle –this results in a moderate other procedures risk - targeted detection risk is 20%. II-6   RP

Additional sample size determination =
Untested Amount/Testing Threshold * Other Procedures Risk Factor

Untested Amount	a)	8,872,569	
÷ Testing Threshold	b)	121,471	73 c)=a)÷b)
* Other Procedures Risk Factor-per table below	d)	2.0	
Additional accounts to be tested:			146 e)=c)*d)

West & Fair, CPAs, LLC uses the following table to determine the *other procedures risk factor*:

Targeted Detection Risk for Accounts Receivable/Sales Cycle From Schedule II-6		*Other Procedures Risk Factor* High	Moderate	Low
Very High	Below 9%	3.0	2.3	2.0
High	10 - 30%	2.7	2.0 d)	1.6
Moderate	31 - 80%	2.3	1.6	1.2
Low	Above 81%	2.0	1.2	1.0

AUDITOR CONCLUSION: The number of accounts receivable confirmed is adequate.

Proli Footwear
Confirmation Summary Worksheet (Selected Responses)
December 31, 2014

Account #	Customer	Balance	Customer Confirm Comments	Auditor Comments	Auditor Action
27136	Harmony Shoe	301,575	sent check dated 12/29/14	Check received 1-4 A-6	None
27116	Big Toe Fashions	22,345	defective merchandise returned November 2014	merchandise in return dept – paper work not processed	
27160	Running Shoes, Inc.	982,313	balance is $795,313; last invoice dated 12/1/2014	JE# 12/25 (B-7) is deemed invalid	
27137	Hot Harvey Puppies	56,189	correct balance is $52,122; billing error due to incorrect prices	Wrong price list used by billing dept	
27133	Fashion Hound	104,411		unable to confirm – 3 requests sent – no reply received – Good credit record	
27180	Toe Poppers	37,188	will try to send partial pay soon	Company entering chapter 7	
27178	Terra Shoes	99,122	we do not owe this - our acct is current	sent to wrong customer-should be TERTA	
27151	Leather Footwear	970,477	balance is $754,477; last invoice dated 12/1/2014	JE# 12/43 (B-7) is deemed invalid	
27159	Planet Venus Shoes	4,766	confirm returned by post office; addressee moved	unable to contact-sales rep says that building is boarded up	
27153	Miracle Heel	75,888	balance correct	over 120 days old; normally slow payer	None

PROLI FOOTWEAR
STAMFORD, CONNECTICUT

January 15, 2015

Big Toe Fashions
Toe Drive
Los Angeles, CA

Dear Sirs:

Our auditors, West & Fair CPAs, LLC, are conducting an audit of our financial statements. Please confirm the balance due at December 31, 2014, which is shown on our records and the enclosed statement as $ 22,345.

Please indicate in the space below whether this is in agreement with your records. If there are differences, please provide any information that will assist our auditors in reconciling the difference. Please also indicate any special sale or payment terms related to this balance.

Please sign and date your response and mail your reply direct to West & Fair CPAs, LLC in the enclosed return envelope. PLEASE DO NOT MAIL PAYMENTS ON YOUR ACCOUNT TO THE AUDITORS.

Very truly yours,

Harold F. Heele
Harold F. Heele,
Vice President – Finance and Chief Financial Officer

To: West & Fair CPAs, LLC

The balance due Proli Footwear of $ 22,345 as of December 31, 2014 is correct with the following exceptions (if any):

Balance is wrong: we returned all merchandise in November. We are waiting to receive credit memo from Proli
_____

Special sale or payment terms (if any):
     none
_____

Signature: *Joe Toe*

Title: *President*   Date: *January 25, 2015*

AUDIT MEMO
West & Fair CPAs, LLC
Stamford, CT

Re: Proli Footwear
Scan of journal entries affecting revenue cycle accounts
Year ended December 31, 2014

In reference to the audit program's Analytic Review Procedure #2, I conducted a scan of those accounts related to the revenue cycle. As part of this procedure, I scanned the following accounts: sales, sales returns and allowances, accounts receivable, and the allowance of Doubtful Accounts. Specifically, I was looking for any entries that might be characterized as unusual and which might result in a material misstatement of the account balances. As part of this review, I identified three adjusting entries that resulted in debits to Accounts Receivable and credits to Sales which require further analysis. They are:

1. 12/2/2014   JE# 12/24: Adjust Account Balances for various billing errors in customer invoices during 2014

   Debit Accounts Receivable........ 343,000
           Credit Sales 343,000

2. 12/4/2015   JE# 12/25: Record unbilled and unrecorded sale to Running Shoes Inc
   Debit Accounts Receivable........ 187,000
           Credit Sales 187,000

3. 12/9/2012   JE# 12/43: Record unbilled and unrecorded sale to Leather Footwear
   Debit Accounts Receivable........ 225,000
           Credit Sales 225,000

I discussed entry 1 (JE# 12/24) with Assistant Controller Brian Baddude and he provided a worksheet analysis supporting the calculation of the sales adjustment amounts that will be billed to the appropriate customers. He says that these billings will be collected without any problem. I recomputed the supporting worksheet and all calculations agree to the journal entry. Further analysis of this data is required.

Entries 2 and 3 (JE #12/25 JE# 12/43) represent adjustments to record unbilled sales of specific customers that were erroneously not invoiced. These amounts were traced to the aged accounts receivable schedule and the amounts are included in the customer balances and the accounts receivable aging schedule total.

Since the physical inventory count was used to determine the cost of sales amount, Baddude indicated that the cost of sales amount shown on the trial balance and financial statements is correctly stated and includes the inventory costs related to these sales.

After my discussion with Baddude, I still have some concerns concerning the appropriateness of these entries and I believe that further audit analysis of these entries should be conducted.

AUDIT MEMO
West & Fair CPAs, LLC
Stamford, CT

Re: Proli Footwear
Review of journal entry exceptions from 2/13/15 Scan of journal entries affecting revenue cycle accounts
Year ended December 31, 2014

After discussion with the Engagement Partner, Richard West and with members of the audit team, I performed further audit analysis of these entries and conclude the following:

1. Concerning entry 1 (JE# 12/24): I vouched the invoices listed to supporting invoices. I was able to find verifiable support for only 7 of the 25 transactions listed. Based on my analysis, it is my opinion that only $52,000 of the $343,000 can be supported; this results in an adjustment of $291,000.

2. Concerning entries 2 and 3 (JE #12/25 JE# 12/43): Shipping documentation was inadequate and did not support shipments to Running Shoes Inc. and Leather Footwear. In reviewing this documentation and related material, I have concluded that these sales transactions recorded by journal entry cannot be supported and should be reversed. I have a question concerning these entries: Do these entries reflect an effort by the Company to increase earnings?

3. Since Cost of Sales was determined by taking a supervised physical inventory, Cost of Sales, subject to other audit adjustments that might be developed in the audit of inventory (assignment 5), is correctly stated and requires no further adjustment even if the accrued sales from entries 2 and 3 (JE #12/25 JE# 12/43) are reversed.

Proli Footwear
Allowance for Doubtful Accounts Worksheet
December 31, 2014

	Allowance Account	Bad Debt Expense
Balance per books - 12/31/2013	$1,760,000	
Add: Monthly recurring entries	880,000	880,000
Subtotal	2,640,000	880,000
Less: Actual write-offs during year	1,540,000	0
Balance per trial balance - 12/31/2014	$1,100,000	$880,000
Audit adjustments:		

Balances before bad debt expense adjustment a)
Required ending balance - *4.3% of adjusted*
         accounts receivable (1)   **b)**
Adjustment required

Balances before bad debt expense adjustment a)
AJE 4-12
Balance per audit - 12/31/2014   **b)**

Adjusted ending accounts receivable balance
Experience ratio   *4.3% (1)*
Required ending allowance balance   **b)**

(1)   *Based on 12/31/2014 analysis of aged accounts receivable, management agrees that the allowance should be adjusted to 4.3% of ending accounts receivable balance. RP*

Proli Footwear
AJE Control – Accounts Receivable and Sales
December 31, 2014

AJE Number	Reference	Accounts/Description	Account Number	Debit	Credit

x = account has impact on income before taxes amount

Impact on income before taxes =   DR/CR

Proli Footwear
Red Flag Events – Accounts Receivable and Sales
December 31, 2014

Event Number	Reference	Auditor Observation

Proli Footwear
Management Letter Comments – Accounts Receivable and Sales
December 31, 2014

Comment Number	Reference	Auditor Observation/ Recommendation	Benefit to Client

Section	Budgeted Time	Time Spent Working with Team	Time Spent Working Alone
4. Accounts Receivable and Sales	6 hours		

Team member names:

ASSIGNMENT #5 – INVENTORY AND ACCOUNTS PAYABLE

ASSIGNMENT

1. Complete each step of the inventory and accounts payable audit program. Indicate completion for each step by making sure that the step is initialed, dated, and that the workpaper reference is indicated. For those audit program steps that are already initialed as having been completed, enter an appropriate date and workpaper reference next to the initials.

2. Be sure to use the appropriate tickmarks to indicate the specific work performed on each piece of audit documentation.

3. Complete and submit for grading all the audit documentation for this section organized in the following sequence:
   a. Audit program with dates, initials and audit documentation references;
   b. Completed Lead Schedule with workpaper references, tickmarks indicating work done and appropriate sign-offs;
   c. Specific audit workpaper schedules in sequence with workpaper references, as appropriate, tickmarks indicating work done and appropriate sign-offs;
   d. Adjusting Journal Entry Control containing the proposed AJEs;
   e. Red Flag Events;
   f. Management Letter Comments containing recommended improvements to internal control and other operating issues;
   g. Updated Time Control Worksheet; and
   h. Updated Working Trial Balance (WTB).

4. Each adjusting entry should be entered on the following audit documentation:
   a. Appropriate workpaper schedule
   b. Lead schedule
   c. AJE control
   d. Working trial balance

AUDIT PROGRAM – INVENTORY AND ACCOUNTS PAYABLE

Procedures	Initials	Date	W/P Ref
General			
1. Foot and crossfoot lead schedule and all other PBC schedules, if any.			
2. Compare balances on other PBC schedules, if any, with balances on lead schedule			
3. Compare balances on lead schedule with account balances in the trial balance.			
Analytical Review Procedures			
1. Note any unusual relationships between current and prior year balances	RP		

Procedures	Initials	Date	W/P Ref

2. Scan for unusual entries to above accounts (e.g., debits to accounts payable from other than check register, etc.). RP

3. Analyze all general journal entries to these accounts. RP

Substantive Audit Procedures – Inventory

1. Review client's inventory-taking instructions. RP 1/2/15

2. Observe physical inventory count.

   a. Make test counts of selected inventory items. RP

   b. Visually examine the raw materials and finished goods inventories for obsolete items. RP

3. Using the physical test counts:

   a. Trace the test counts to the physical inventory tag control.

   b. Trace the test counts from the inventory tag control to the inventory count sheet summary.

4. On a test basis, vouch the number of units and the inventory description from the physical inventory tag control to the physical inventory tag. RP

5. Using client's inventory count sheet summary:

   a. Verify arithmetic accuracy.

   b. Test unit prices to recent vendor invoices. RP 2/15 C-17

   c. Agree total per PBC schedule to trial balance.

   d. Suggest write-off of any inventory with no sales within the previous 12 months

6. Perform purchase cutoff tests for potential inventory in transit.

   a. Examine purchase cutoff analysis to determine that inventory purchases are recorded in the proper period.

   b. Review vendors' invoices in the purchase journal, or voucher register, for several days before and after year-end, and compare with receiving reports. RP

   c. Review purchase returns after year-end for proper authorization and recording, and compare with supporting documentation (shipping records, memoranda, etc.). RP

7. Inquire whether any inventory is located off premises (i.e., consigned out). RP

Procedures	Initials	Date	W/P Ref

8. Inquire whether any inventory is pledged or if any purchase commitments exist. RP

9. Determine proper financial statement classification and disclosure. RP

Substantive Audit Procedures - Accounts Payable (Trade)

1. Determine if appropriate to request positive confirmations from selected vendors. RP 1/4/15

2. Review the replies on the confirmation summary schedule and prepare any necessary adjusting entries.

3. On a test basis:
   a. Examine completeness of vouchers, noting purchase orders, receiving reports, invoices, and copies of checks. Check for proper destruction to prohibit resubmission for duplicate payment. RP
   b. Trace payment to check register. RP
   c. Note proper approvals. RP

4. Make inquiries regarding the existence and the substance of any related party transactions RP

HELPFUL HINTS FROM THE IN-CHARGE ACCOUNTANT:

1. Use a tickmark to show each work procedure performed.
2. Remember to post adjusting entries affecting the inventory and accounts payable section from the previous sections to the inventory and accounts payable lead sheet.
3. Be alert for "Red Flag" events. A red flag event is an event or transaction that might indicate fraudulent activity, but needs further investigation to determine:
   a. Whether it was intentional or just human error and
   b. The impact of the event.
4. Make sure that you review the accounts receivable and sales audit documentation for any inventory effects.
5. FOB refers to the point at which the title for goods being purchased by Proli transfer to Proli from the vendor.
6. The inventory balances per the books (on the trial balance) and the lead schedule reflect all inventories physically on hand at Proli facilities on 12/31/14 and counted during the physical inventory count taken on 1/2/15 pursuant to the detail in the supporting audit documentation.
7. Remember that any work RP has completed need not be repeated by you. You may assume that RP has done all the necessary work to complete the work program step correctly. All of RP's work looks like this.

Proli Footwear
Lead Schedule - Inventory and Accounts Payable
December 31, 2014

Account Number	Account Title	Balance per T/B Debit	Balance per T/B Credit	- - - - Adjustments - - - - Debit	- - - - Adjustments - - - - Credit	Balance per Audit Debit	Balance per Audit Credit
1310	Raw Materials	6,550,104					
1315	Work in Process	0					
1320	Finished Goods	37,117,696					
	Total Inventory	43,667,800					
2300	Accounts Payable – Trade		3,815,900				
6000	Cost of Goods Sold	108,711,900					

Impact of AJEs for this assignment on net income before income taxes =   DR/CR

72

AUDIT MEMO
West & Fair CPAs, LLC
Stamford, CT

Re: Proli Footwear
Inventory Observation
December 31, 2014

I was present during the physical inventory count on January 2, 2015 at the Proli, CT facilities.

I made test counts of the client's shoe inventory on hand at January 2, 2015 (see schedule C-8).

I made test counts of supplies on hand at January 2, 2015 and traced these counts to the client's summary sheets.

I noticed that the total inventory of 8,500 yards of ostrich leather (C-5) valued at $131,750 was completely covered with dust in an unopened package. The client stated that production using ostrich leather stopped two years ago due to low sales volume and the ostrich leather was retained in inventory because they thought that it might be used again sometime in the future.

The client stopped production on 12/20/14. There was no work-in-progress noted in the factory or warehouse. The last 5 receiving reports (C-11) issued in 2015 are as follows:

> #1158 on 12/28 from Scuff GB Leather
> #1159 on 12/28 from Brazilian Leather Works
> #1160 on 12/29 from Footwear Warehouse
> #1161 on 12/29 from Formal Fabrics
> #1162 on 12/29 from Kyoto Leather

I examined all these items and determined that they were included in the physical inventory count. No receiving reports have been issued since 12/29/14.

The client costs the inventories on a first-in, first-out (FIFO) basis, so it is important to check some year-end vendor invoices for prices to be used in year-end inventory valuation.

AUDIT MEMO
West & Fair CPAs, LLC
Stamford, CT

Re: Proli Footwear
Inventory Observation
December 31, 2014

I was present during the physical inventory count on January 2, 2015 at the Waterbury, CT facilities.

I made test counts of the client's shoe inventory on hand at January 2, 2015 (see schedule C-9).

I made test counts of supplies on hand at January 2, 2015 and traced these counts to the client's summary sheets.

The client stopped production on 12/20/15. There was no work-in-progress noted in the factory or warehouse. No receiving reports have been issued since 12/20/15.

....

AUDIT MEMO
West & Fair CPAs, LLC
Stamford, CT

Re: Proli Footwear
Inventory Observation
December 31, 2014

I was present during the physical inventory count on January 2, 2015 at the Walton, FL facilities.

I made test counts of the client's shoe inventory on hand at January 2, 2015 (see schedule C-10).

I made test counts of supplies on hand at January 2, 2015 and traced these counts to the client's summary sheets.

The client stopped production on 12/20/14. There was no work-in-progress noted in the factory or warehouse. No receiving reports have been issued since 12/20/14.

Proli Footwear
Count Sheet Summary - Inventory
December 31, 2014

Finished Goods Summary - All Locations

Item	Units	Unit Cost	Total
Proli A	88,729	91	8,074,339
Proli B	68,128	72	4,905,216
Dapper	36,209	141	5,105,469
Icetemp	57,833	72	4,163,976
Leatherworker	57,991	66	3,827,406
Litetech	75,615	52	3,931,980
Mudhoppers	54,425	36	1,959,300
Sportech	37,205	64	2,381,120
Woodland	37,930	73	2,768,890
Totals	514,065		37,117,696

Raw Materials Summary - All Locations

Vinyl		1,035,802
Rubber		1,036,200
Leather		
Cowhide	1,511,800	
Ostrich	131,750	
Pigskin	1,168,303	2,811,853
Chemicals		942,810
Thread		236,801
Adhesives		486,638
Totals		6,550,104

Total inventory before audit adjustments — 43,667,800

Audit adjustments:

Balance per audit

<table>
<tr><td colspan="3">Proli Footwear
Physical Inventory Tag Control
December 31, 2014</td></tr>
</table>

Tag #	Item Description	Count (units)
Proli, CT Location:		
101	Dapper	3,610
102	Dapper	6,009
103	Dapper	7,052
104	Dapper ∨	4,065
105	Dapper	6,074
106	Sportech	11,839
107	Sportech	5,961
108	Icetemp	9,197
109	Icetemp	15,237
110	Woodland	10,036
111	Void	------
112	Woodland	8,312
113	Woodland	7,950
114	Litetech	21,896
115	Proli A ∨	23,229
116	Proli A	21,064
117	Void	------
118	Proli A	24,396
119	Proli B	22,884
120	Proli B ∨	26,279
121	Sportech	1,674
122	Proli B	18,965
123	Proli A	9,875
124	Litetech	9,845
125	Void ∨	------
126	Proli A	10,165
127	Dapper	9,399
128	Woodland	11,632

<table>
<tr><td colspan="3">Proli Footwear
Physical Inventory Tag Control
December 31, 2014</td></tr>
</table>

Tag #	Item Description	Count (units)
Waterbury, CT Location:		
201	Icetemp ∨	6,537
202	Icetemp	12,368
203	Icetemp	14,494
204	Void	------
205	Mudhoppers ∨	18,839
206	Mudhoppers	23,599
207	Mudhoppers	11,987
Walton, FL Location:		
301	Sportech ∨	4,989
302	Sportech	4,849
303	Litetech	17,963
304	Leatherworker	17,315
305	Leatherworker	9,525
306	Void	------
307	Leatherworker	9,688
308	Leatherworker	11,301
309	Void	------
310	Sportech	7,893
311	Leatherworker	11,962
312	Litetech ∨	25,911

∨ = Vouched number of units and inventory description to physical inventory count tag. RP

Proli Footwear
Raw Materials by Vendor - All Locations
December 31, 2014

Vinyl			
Vijay Vinyl Supply	789,229		
Formal Fabrics	246,573		
Total Vinyl			1,035,802
Rubber			
Dryer Industries	677,921		
Indio's Rubber Supply	99,562		
Thailand National Rubber	258,717		
Total Rubber			1,036,200
Leather			
Cowhide			
Aukland Leather	277,697		
Brazilian Leather Works	239,615		
Kalispell Leather	293,965		
Lincoln Leather	324,130		
Scuff GB Leather	376,393 *C-16*		
Total Cowhide		1,511,800	
Ostrich			
African Leather Producer		131,750	
Pigskin			
Elfriede's Famous Fabrics		1,168,303	
Total Leather			2,811,853
Chemicals			
Carlisle Chemicals	405,240		
Conn Chemical Co	537,570		
Total Chemicals			942,810
Thread			
Mary's Supply House	190,700		
Thelma's Threads	46,101		
Total Thread			236,801
Adhesives			
Standard Adhesive	322,527		
Veritech Adhesives	164,111		
Total Adhesives			486,638

Proli Footwear
Inventory Test Counts - Proli, CT Location
December 31, 2014

Tag #	Item Description	Count
124	Litetech	9,845
109	Icetemp	15,237
127	Dapper	9,399
112	Woodland	8,312
103	Dapper	7,052
115	Proli A	23,229
118	Proli A	24,396
106	Sportech	11,839

Proli Footwear
Inventory Test Counts - Waterbury, CT Location
December 31, 2014

Tag #	Item Description	Count
203	Icetemp	14,494
206	Mudhoppers	23,599

Proli Footwear
Inventory Test Counts - Walton, FL Location
December 31, 2014

Tag #	Item Description	Count
303	Litetech	17,963
307	Leatherworker	9,688
311	Leatherworker	11,962

Proli Footwear
Purchase Cut-Off Analysis - December 31, 2014

Receiving Report #	Receiving Report Date	Received from	Raw Materials Inventory #1310	Accounts Payable #2300	Other	Purchase Journal Date	Comments	Auditor Action
C-2 1158	12/28/14	Scuff GB Leather	36,665	36,665		12/29/14	Shipped FOB shipping point on 12/20/2014; counted in inventory; included in Acc Pay	
C-2 1159	12/28/14	Brazilian Leather Works	95,321	95,321		01/06/15	Shipped FOB destination on 12/7/14; counted in inventory; purchase recorded after 12/31/2013 C-14	
C-2 1160	12/29/14	Footwear Warehouse			22,581	N/A	Customer overstock; returned to finished goods warehouse on 12/29/2014; included in physical inventory count	
C-2 1161	12/29/14	Formal Fabrics	27,860	27,860		12/30/14	counted in inventory	
C-2 1162	12/29/14	Kyoto Leather	80,431	80,431		12/30/14	Shipped FOB shipping point on 12/5/14; counted in inventory	
1163	1/4/15	Vinyl Magic	59,399	59,399		01/05/15	Shipped FOB destination on 1/2/15	
1164	1/4/15	Rubber Wholesalers	63,692	63,692		01/05/15	Shipped FOB shipping point on 12/31/14	
1165	1/4/15	Adhesives Inc.	89,894	89,894		01/06/15	Shipped FOB destination on 1/2/15	
1166	1/6/15	Kalispell Leather	59,419	59,419		01/06/15	Shipped FOB destination on 1/2/15	
1167	1/6/15	Vinyl Magic	57,177	57,177		01/07/15	Shipped FOB destination on 1/2/15	
1168	1/6/15	Indio's Rubber Supply	36,083	36,083		01/07/15	Shipped FOB destination on 1/4/15	
1169	1/8/15	Thelma's Threads	48,028	48,028		01/09/15	Shipped FOB destination on 1/2/15	
1170	1/8/15	Veritech Adhesives	56,350	56,350		01/09/15	Shipped FOB destination on 1/4/15	
1171	1/8/15	Conn Chemical Co.	79,599	79,599		01/09/15	Shipped FOB destination on 1/7/15	

Proli Footwear
Summary of Accounts Payable - Trade
December 31, 2014

Vendor			Accounts Payable Balance		Purchases During Year
Aukland Leather	C		99,509		2,557,822
Brazilian Leather Works	C	A	191,240		1,790,000
BZ Leather	C	A	122,778		7,875,547
Carlisle Chemicals	C		90,994		719,446
Conn Chemical Co	C		74,038		1,546,849
Elfriede's Famous Fabrics	C	A	389,801		2,594,627
Formal Fabrics	C		92,455		520,214
Dryer Industries, Inc.	C	A	186,430		9,487,600
Indio's Rubber Supply	C	A	213,849		6,281,408
Kalispell Leather	C	A	352,493		1,195,994
Kyoto Leather	C	A	405,789		7,628,757
Lincoln Leather	C	A	135,399		5,532,207
Mary's Supply House	C		0		2,187,491
Marie's Supplies	C		104,978		3,476,843
Midwest Leather	C		99,052		2,510,019
Nebraska Leather	C	A	199,605		4,134,781
Scuff GB Leather	C	A	126,935	C-16	3,812,851
Standard Adhesive	C		65,957		4,989,718
Thailand National Rubber Co.	C		58,458		3,229,329
Thelma's Threads	C		99,638		3,065,312
Veritech Adhesives	C		42,842		2,834,819
Vijay Vinyl Supply	C		107,503		3,394,178
Other 19 confirmed accounts	C		184,949		6,537,372
Other 285 accounts not confirmed			371,208		22,033,888
Totals - 326 accounts			3,815,900		109,937,072

C = Confirmation sent to vendor.

A = Balance over testing threshold

Proli Footwear
Determination of Sample Size for Substantive Tests of Accounts Payable
Using a Formal Nonstatistical Sampling Plan
December 31, 2014

	Number of Vendors	Amount
Tolerable misstatement for each account balance:		
Testing threshold: West & Fair, CPAs, LLC uses 1/3 of tolerable misstatement		b)
Accounts Payable Balance:		
Accounts exceeding threshold:		
Unusual items:		
Large debit balances		
Vendor accounts in dispute		
Vendor names that cause concern		
Untested amount		a)
Additional accounts tested	e)	
Total accounts tested		

It has been determined that a low level of reliance can be placed on other audit procedures for accounts payable - this results in a high other procedures risk-targeted detection risk is 4% II-6 RP

Additional sample size determination =
Untested Amount/Testing Threshold * Other Procedures Risk Factor

Untested Amount	a)	
÷ Testing Threshold	b)	c) = a) * b)
* Other Procedures Risk Factor-per table below	d)	
Additional accounts tested (rounded)		e) = c) * d)

West & Fair, CPAs, LLC uses the *following table to determine the other procedures risk factor:*

Targeted Detection Risk for Accounts Payable/Purchases Cycle *Other Procedures Risk Factor*

From Schedule II-6		High	Moderate	Low
Very High	Below 9%	3.0 d)	2.3	2.0
High	10 - 30%	2.7	2.0	1.6
Moderate	31 - 80%	2.3	1.6	1.2
Low	Above 81%	2.0	1.2	1.0

AUDITOR CONCLUSION:

NOTE TO STUDENTS: If you believe that the number of items tested is inadequate, state the minimum additional amount to be tested in your conclusion. You should assume that RP will do the additional testing.

Proli Footwear
Accounts Payable - Trade
Confirmation Summary (selected responses)
December 31, 2014

Vendor	Balance Per Books	Vendor Confirm Comments	Auditor Comments	Auditor Action
Brazilian Leather Works	191,240	Balance is $286,561	Goods included in physical inventory not recorded as payable; difference=$95,321 C-11	
Conn Chemical	74,038	Balance is correct		
Elfriede's Famous Fabrics	389,801	Balance is correct		
Indio's Rubber Supply	213,849	Balance is correct		
Mary's Supply House	0	Balance is $(15,298)	Proli paid same invoice twice; vendor balance is correct	
Midwest Leather	99,052	Balance is correct		
Nebraska Leather	199,605	Balance is over 90 days past due	Partial payment made on 1/14/2015 for 25,000 A-7	
Scuff GB Leather	126,935	Balance is correct	It appears that prices charged by Scuff GB Leather are 25% higher than other leather vendors; RP investigating related party issue.	
Standard Adhesives	65,957	Balance is $65,957		
Vijay Vinyl Supply	107,503	Balance is over 60 days past due	Partial payment made on 1/5/2015 for 85,900 A-7	

PROLI FOOTWEAR
STAMFORD, CONNECTICUT

January 15, 2015

Attn: Joan Scuff
Scuff GB Leather
5 Ostentatious Lane
Candleweed Lake, CT

Dear Sirs:

Our independent auditors, West & Fair CPAs, LLC, are performing an audit of our financial statements. For this reason, please inform them in the space provided below the amount, if any, owed to you by this company at December 31, 2014.

Please attach an itemized statement supporting any balance owed, showing all unpaid items. Your reply should be sent directly to West & Fair CPAs, LLC in the enclosed return envelope.

Very truly yours,

Harold F. Heele
Harold F. Heele,
Vice President – Finance and Chief Financial Officer

To: West & Fair CPAs, LLC

Our records show that the amount of $ 26,935 was owed to us by Proli Footwear at December 31, 2014 as shown by the itemized statement attached.

Signature: *Joan Scuff*   Date: *1/20/15*
Title: President

AUDIT MEMO
West & Fair CPAs, LLC
Stamford, CT

Re: Proli Footwear
Goodwin Buye Termination

Goodwin Buye, VP of Purchasing, has been purchasing leather products from Scuff GB Leather at approximately 25% above market rates. Scuff GB Leather is owned and managed by Goodwin Buye's wife, Joan Scuff. This scheme was recently discovered as a result of the ongoing audit work led by RP and was reported to the Board of Directors' Audit Committee a few weeks ago. As a result of these revelations, the Board of Directors has conducted an investigation and has found that Goodwin Buye and Scuff GB Leather have been covertly conducting above-market, related party purchase transactions for about 3 years.

As a result of the Board's findings, the employment of Goodwin Buye has been terminated with cause and the Company plans to pursue civil fraud violations against Goodwin Buye and Joan Scuff in an effort to recover the losses incurred by the Proli as a result of their scheme.

The amount of the loss resulting from the above-market transactions occurring in 2014 needs to be determined and an adjustment proposed. At the present time, it has been determined that the total purchases from Scuff in 2014 amount to $3,812,851 *C-12* of which $126,935 *C-12* remain unpaid in Accounts Payable at December 31, 2014. The Company will not pay this remaining balance because of this fraud loss. Of the total purchases from Scuff in 2014 ($3,812, 851 C-12), $376,303 C-7 is still in ending inventory at the above market cost. Therefore an adjusting entry will need to be prepared to reverse out the related party overpricing and to record the related party fraud loss net of the ending accounts payable. In addition, it must be decided how the prior year losses should be handled in accordance with the adjustment discussion shown below. The client has been asked to provide a list of raw materials purchases by vendor to determine the amount of raw materials that still remain in raw materials inventory.

Losses that occurred in prior years are estimated to be as follows:

- 2013.....................$657,000
- 2012.....................$566,000

The related party fraud occurred over a 3 year period so a choice will have to be made whether to use the "rollover method," which is an income statement approach, or the" iron curtain method," which is a balance sheet approach, will be used when making the adjustment. The audit team should discuss which method is appropriate.

Proli Footwear
Costs and Selling Prices of Products
December 31, 2014

Product		Cost	Selling Price
Proli A	V	91	125
Proli B	V	72	105
Dapper	V	141	235
Icetemp	V	72	108
Leatherworker	V	66	85
Litetech	V	52	70
Mudhoppers	V	36	45
Sportech	V	64	80
Woodland	V	73	115

V = vouched cost to cost records

Proli Footwear
AJE Control-Inventory and Accounts Payable
December 31, 2014

AJE Number	Reference	Accounts/Description	Account Number	Debit	Credit

x = account has impact on income before taxes amount

Impact on income before taxes =   DR/CR

Proli Footwear
Red Flag Events-Inventory and Accounts Payable
December 31, 2014

Event Number	Reference	Auditor Observation

Proli Footwear
Management Letter Comments-Inventory and Accounts Payable
December 31, 2014

Comment Number	Reference	Auditor Observation/ Recommendation	Benefit to Client

Proli Footwear
Time Control
December 31, 2014

Section	Budgeted Time	Time Spent Working with Team	Time Spent Working Alone
5. Inventory and Accounts Payable	7 hours		

Team member names:

ASSIGNMENT #6A – PROPERTY, PLANT, AND EQUIPMENT

ASSIGNMENT

1. Complete each step of the property, plant, and equipment audit program. Indicate completion for each step by making sure that the step is initialed, dated, and that the workpaper reference is indicated. For those audit program steps that are already initialed as having been completed, enter an appropriate date and workpaper reference next to the initials.

2. Be sure to use the appropriate tickmarks to indicate the specific work performed on each piece of audit documentation.

3. Complete and submit for grading all the audit documentation for this section organized in the following sequence:
   a. Audit program with dates, initials and audit documentation references;
   b. Completed Lead Schedule with workpaper references, tickmarks indicating work done and appropriate sign-offs;
   c. Specific audit workpaper schedules in sequence with workpaper references, as appropriate, tickmarks indicating work done and appropriate sign-offs;
   d. Adjusting Journal Entry Control containing the proposed AJEs;
   e. Red Flag Events;
   f. Management Letter Comments containing recommended improvements to internal control and other operating issues;
   g. Updated Time Control Worksheet; and
   h. Updated Working Trial Balance (WTB).

4. Each adjusting entry should be entered on the following audit documentation:
   a. Appropriate workpaper schedule
   b. Lead schedule
   c. AJE control
   d. Working trial balance

AUDIT PROGRAM – PROPERTY, PLANT, AND EQUIPMENT

Procedures	Initials	Date	W/P Ref
General			
1. Foot and crossfoot lead schedule and all other PBC schedules			
2. Compare balances on other PBC schedules with balances on lead schedule.			
3. Compare balances on lead schedules with account balances in the trial balance.			
4. Understand client posting regarding:			
a. Minimum amount to capitalize.			
b. Depreciation in year of acquisition and disposition.			

Procedures	Initials	Date	W/P Ref

Analytical Review

1. Review general ledger accounts, noting any unusual entries. — RP 2/15

2. Review minutes for authorization for acquisitions and disposals, if appropriate. — RP 2/15 DA-2-6 and DA-11

Substantive Procedures

1. Recompute/complete depreciation schedule for the current and all prior years.

2. Compare acquisitions and dispositions with underlying documentation, noting differences, if any. Trace such transactions to cash disbursements and cash receipts. — RP

3. Review supporting documentation of entries to the repairs and maintenance expense account.

4. Review supporting documentation of entries to the gain/loss on disposal of long-lived assets account. — RP

5. Review insurance coverage in comparison to replacement or current plant, property, and equipment values. — RP

HELPFUL HINTS FROM THE IN-CHARGE ACCOUNTANT:

1. Use a tickmark to show each work procedure performed.

2. Remember to post adjusting entries affecting the property, plant and, equipment section from the previous sections to the property, plant, and equipment lead sheet.

3. Be alert for "Red Flag" events. A red flag event is an event or transaction that might indicate fraudulent activity, but needs further investigation to determine:
   a. Whether it was intentional or just human error and
   b. The impact of the event.

4. Refer to an accounting text and read about prior period adjustments. Remember that prior period adjustments occur when income statement/retained earning adjustments are proposed after the books have been closed. Remember to include income tax effects, if appropriate. All deferred tax liabilities and assets should be recorded in Account # 2700. The Company's combined federal and state income tax rate is 40%.

5. When making the adjusting entries for schedules D-2, make a separate net adjusting entry for each asset group (i.e. buildings, leased buildings, manufacturing equipment, etc.)

6. For this simulation, assume that book and tax depreciation are the same for all buildings, leased buildings, manufacturing equipment, warehouse equipment, and office equipment.

7. Proli uses the half year convention for depreciation. Make sure that only one-half year's depreciation is taken in the year of purchase and the one-half in the year of disposal.

8. Remember that any work RP has completed need not be repeated by you. You may assume that RP has done <u>all</u> the necessary work to complete the work program step correctly. All of RP's work looks like this.

Proli Footwear
Lead Schedule - Long-Lived Assets - Property, Plant, and Equipment
December 31, 2014

Account Number	Account Title	Balance per T/B Debit	Balance per T/B Credit	Adjustments Debit	Adjustments Credit	Balance per Audit Debit	Balance per Audit Credit
1511	Land	1,879,000					
1512	Buildings	3,464,840					
1513	Leased Buildings	3,489,988					
1521	Manufacturing Equipment	14,992,700					
1522	Warehouse Equipment	13,795,400					
1523	Office Equipment	3,539,800					
	Accumulated Depreciation:						
1531	Buildings		3,534,647				
1532	Leased Buildings		2,708,170				
1533	Manufacturing Equipment		12,693,959				
1534	Warehouse Equipment		4,909,542				
1535	Office Equipment		1,934,198				

Proli Footwear
Lead Schedule - Long-Lived Assets - Property, Plant, and Equipment
December 31, 2014

Account Number	Account Title	Balance per T/B Debit	Credit	Adjustments Debit	Credit	Balance per Audit Debit	Credit
Depreciation Expense:							
7201	Buildings	1,476,213					
7202	Leased Buildings	310,330					
7203	Manufacturing Equipment	594,320					
7204	Warehouse Equipment	714,003					
7205	Office Equipment	306,165					
Related Accounts:							
7380	Repairs and Maintenance	930,464					
8100	Gain/Loss on Sale Plant Assets	0					

Impact of AJEs for this assignment on client's net income before income taxes = _____ DR/CR

93

Proli Footwear
Depreciation Schedule
December 31, 2014

Description	Method Used	Year Acquired		Cost	Accumulated Depreciation 2012	Expense 2013	Accumulated Depreciation 2013	Expense 2014	Accumulated Depreciation 2014
Buildings: PER BOOKS									
Proli, CT building DA-7	SL 35 years	1996	M	1,087,650	512,749	31,076	543,825	31,076	574,901 cf
Walton, FL building DA-7	SL 35 years	2001	M	631,900	207,624	18,054	225,678	18,054	243,732 cf
Walton, FL building DA-7	SL 35 years	2011	M	460,290	19,727	13,151	32,878	13,151	46,029 cf
Proli, CT building DA-7	SL 35 years	2014	M	1,285,000	0	1,256,053	1,256,053	1,413,932	2,669,985 cf
Totals (a)			DA-1	3,464,840	740,100	1,318,334	2,058,434	1,476,213	3,534,647 cf
				f	f	f	f	f DA-1	f DA-1
Buildings: PER AUDITORS									
Proli, CT building	SL 35 years	1996		1,087,650	512,749	31,076	543,825	31,076	574,901 cf
Walton, FL building	SL 35 years	2001		631,900	207,624	18,054	225,678	18,054	243,732 cf
Walton, FL building	SL 35 years	2011		460,290	19,727	13,151	32,878	13,151	46,029 cf
Proli, CT building	SL 35 years	2014		1,285,000	0	0	0	18,357	18,357 cf
Totals (b)				3,464,840	740,100	62,281	802,381	80,638	883,019 cf
				f	f	f	f	f	f
Correction needed = (b) - (a)				0	0	(1,256,053)	(1,256,053)	(1,395,575)	(2,651,628)

M = Traced authorization to lease facilities to the Board of Directors' minutes

94

Proli Footwear
Depreciation Schedule
December 31, 2014

Description	Method Used	Year Acquired	Cost	Accumulated Depreciation 2012	Expense 2013	Accumulated Depreciation 2013	Expense 2014	Accumulated Depreciation 2014
Leased Buildings: PER BOOKS (1)								
Lease L1	DA-8 SL 30 years	2001	1,042,810	599,616	52,141	651,757	52,141	703,898
Lease L2A	DA-8 SL 10 years	2006	943,406	613,214	94,341	707,555	94,341	801,896
Lease L4	DA-8 SL 14 years	2001	1,064,826	874,679	76,059	950,738	76,059	1,026,797
Lease L5	DA-8 SL 5 years	2012	438,946	43,895	43,895	87,790	87,789	175,579
Totals			3,489,988	2,131,404	266,436	2,397,840	310,330	2,708,170
Leased Buildings: PER AUDITORS (1)								
Lease L1	SL 30 years	2001	1,042,810	342,244	29,760	372,004	29,760	401,764
Lease L2A	SL 10 years	2006	943,406	548,214	84,341	632,555	84,341	716,896
Lease L4	SL 14 years	2001	1,064,826	751,464	65,345	816,809	65,345	882,154
Lease L5	SL 5 years	2012	438,946	36,395	72,789	109,184	72,789	181,973
Totals			3,489,988	1,678,317	252,235	1,930,552	252,235	2,182,787

Correction needed =

(1) Classification of leased property and verification of lease terms has not been performed.
    This work will be done in the Liabilities section. RP

M = Traced authorization to lease facilities to the Board of Directors' minutes

Proli Footwear
Depreciation Schedule
December 31, 2014

Description		Method Used	Year Acquired	Cost	Accumulated Depreciation 2012	Expense 2013	Accumulated Depreciation 2013	Expense 2014	Accumulated Depreciation 2014
Manufacturing Equipment: PER BOOKS									
Various	DA-7 M	DDB 15 years	1996	6,254,980	6,096,524	31,691	6,128,215	25,353	6,153,568
Various	DA-7 M	DDB 15 years	2001	5,703,420	2,147,380	711,208	2,858,588	568,966	3,427,554
Various	DA-7 M	DDB 15 years	2013	2,792,000	2,510,237	0	2,510,237	0	2,510,237
Various	DA-7 M	DDB 15 years	2014	242,300	602,600	0	602,600	0	602,600
Totals				14,992,700	11,356,741	742,899	12,099,640	594,319	12,693,959

Manufacturing Equipment: PER AUDITORS				
Various	DDB 15 years	1996	6,254,980
Various	DDB 15 years	2001	5,703,420
Various	DDB 15 years	2013	2,792,000
Various	DDB 15 years	2014	242,300
Totals			14,992,700

Correction needed =

M = Traced authorization to lease facilities to the Board of Directors' minutes

Proli Footwear
Depreciation Schedule
December 31, 2014

Description	Method Used	Year Acquired		Cost	Accumulated Depreciation 2012	Expense 2013	Accumulated Depreciation 2013	Expense 2014	Accumulated Depreciation 2014
Warehouse Equipment: PER BOOKS									
Various DA-7	SL 15 years	2001	M	1,983,450	1,520,645	132,230	1,652,875	132,230	1,785,105 cf
Various DA-7	SL 15 years	2005	M	1,545,000	763,958	103,000	866,958	103,000	969,958 cf
Various DA-7	SL 15 years	2010	M	7,181,600	1,196,933	478,773	1,675,706	478,773	2,154,479 cf
Various DA-7	SL 15 years	2013	M	585,350	0	0	0	0	0 cf
Various DA-7	SL 15 years	2014	M	2,500,000	0	0	0	0	0 cf
Totals			DA-1	13,795,400	3,481,536	714,003	4,195,539	714,003	4,909,542 cf
				f	f	f	f	f	DA-1
Warehouse Equipment: PER AUDITORS									
Various	SL 15 years	2001		1,983,450	1,520,645	132,230	1,652,875	132,230	1,785,105 cf
Various	SL 15 years	2005		1,545,000	772,500	103,000	875,500	103,000	978,500 cf
Various	SL 15 years	2010		7,181,600	1,196,933	478,773	1,675,706	478,773	2,154,479 cf
Various	SL 15 years	2013		585,350	0	19,512	19,512	39,023	58,535 cf
Various	SL 15 years	2014		2,500,000	0	0	0	83,333	83,333 cf
Totals				13,795,400	3,490,078	733,515	4,223,593	836,359	5,059,952 cf
				f	f	f	f	f	f

Correction needed =

M = Traced authorization to lease facilities to the Board of Directors' minutes

97

Proli Footwear
Depreciation Schedule
December 31, 2014

Description		Method Used	Year Acquired		Cost	Accumulated Depreciation 2012	Expense 2013	Accumulated Depreciation 2013	Expense 2014	Accumulated Depreciation 2014
Office Equipment: PER BOOKS										
Various	DA-7	SL 10 years	2004	M	450,000	292,500	45,000	337,500	45,000	382,500 cf
Various	DA-7	SL 10 years	2005	M	329,850	181,418	32,985	214,403	32,985	247,388 cf
Various	DA-7	SL 10 years	2006	M	1,387,500	624,375	138,750	763,125	138,750	901,875 cf
Various	DA-7	SL 10 years	2008	M	894,300	223,575	89,430	313,005	89,430	402,435 cf
Various	DA-7	SL 10 years	2011	M	478,150	0	0	0	0	0 cf
Totals			DA-1		3,539,800	1,321,868	306,165	1,628,033	306,165	1,934,198 cf DA-1
					f	f	f	f	f DA-1 f	f
Office Equipment: PER AUDITORS										
Various		SL 10 years	2004		450,000	292,500	45,000	337,500	45,000	382,500 cf
Various		SL 10 years	2005		329,850	181,418	32,985	214,403	32,985	247,388 cf
Various		SL 10 years	2006		1,387,500	624,375	138,750	763,125	138,750	901,875 cf
Various		SL 10 years	2008		894,300	223,575	89,430	313,005	89,430	402,435 cf
Various		SL 10 years	2011		478,150	0	23,908	23,908	47,815	71,723 cf
Totals					3,539,800	1,321,868	330,073	1,651,941	353,980	2,005,921 cf
					f	f	f	f	f	f

Correction needed =

M = Traced authorization to lease facilities to the Board of Directors' minutes

98

©Proctor and Poli

Proli Footwear
Depreciation Policy
December 31, 2014

Account Title	Method	Useful Life	Salvage Value
Buildings	Straight-line	35 years	0
Leased Buildings	Straight-line	lease term	varies by lease See DA-8
Manufacturing Equipment	Double declining balance	15 years	0
Warehouse Equipment	Straight-line	15 years	0
Office Equipment	Straight-line	10 years	0

Note 1: Per the client's policy and procedures manual, in the year of acquisition and disposal, 1/2 year depreciation is taken. RP

Note 2: Per the client's policy and procedures manual, any individual item exceeding $1,000 in value is to be capitalized. RP

Note 3: Book and tax bases are the same for all buildings, leased buildings, and equipment (i.e. book depreciation = tax depreciation).

Proli Footwear
Lease Information
December 31, 2014

Location	Lease ID	Principal Uses	Lease term	Years	Guaranteed Residual Value	Cost per books (1)		Type of lease per books
Proli, Ct	L1	Principal sales, marketing and executive offices	2001-2031	30	150,000	1,042,810	M	Capital
Proli, Ct	L2A	Main warehouse and distribution facility	2006-2016	10	100,000	943,406	M	Capital
Proli, Ct	L2B	Main warehouse and distribution facility	year-to-year	n/a	0	N/A	M	Operating
Walton, FL	L3	Warehouse and distribution facility	2001-2016	15	100,000	N/A	M	Operating
Waterbury, CT	L4	Warehouse and distribution facility	2001-2015	14	150,000	1,064,826	M	Capital
Waterbury, CT	L5	Manufacturing, warehousing and offices for Mudhoppers, Inc.	2012-2017	5	75,000	438,946	M	Capital

M = Traced authorization to lease facilities to the Board of Directors' minutes

Note: At the inception of the lease, the Company had no intention of retaining ownership at the end of the lease. RP

(1) Cost represents the present value of the minimum lease payments at the inception of the lease. RP

NOTE TO STUDENTS: The classification of the leases as capital or operating is tested in Assignment 7 (EB-2-EB-7). In this assignment presume that the client's classification is correct.

100

Proli Footwear
Determination of Sample Size for Substantive Tests of Property, Plant and Equipment
Using a Formal Nonstatistical Sampling Plan
December 31, 2014

	Number of Items	Amount
Tolerable misstatement for each account balance:		
Testing threshold: West & Fair, CPAs, LLC uses 1/3 of tolerable misstatement		d)
Long-Lived Assets Balance:	a) 217	
Less: Items exceeding threshold:	b)	
Less: Unusual items:		
Additions involving interest capitalization		
Untested items		E)
Additional items tested	c)	g)
Total items tested		

It has been determined that a moderate level of reliance can be placed on other audit procedures for long-lived assets - this results in a moderate other procedures risk –targeted detection risk is 60% II-6   RP

Additional sample size determination =
Untested Items/Testing Threshold * Other Procedures Risk Factor

Untested items	E)
÷ Testing Threshold	d)
* Other Procedures Risk Factor-per table below f)	
Additional items to be tested:	c)

West & Fair, CPAs, LLC uses the following table to determine the
other procedures risk factor:

Targeted Detection Risk for Long-Lived Assets From Schedule II-5		Other Procedures Risk Factor		
		High	Moderate	Low
Very High	Below 9%	3.0	2.3	2.0
High	10 - 30%	2.7	2.0	1.6
Moderate	31 - 80%	2.3	1.6 f)	1.2
Low	Above 81%	2.0	1.2	1.0

Property, Plant, Equipment	Total Items	Above Threshold		Additional Testing	
		Items	Cost	Items	Cost
Land	4 items	4	1,879,000	0	
Buildings	4 items	4	3,464,840	0	
Leased Buildings	4 items	4	3,489,988	0	
Manufacturing Equipment	25 items	14	13,820,430	4	448,960
Warehouse Equipment	15 items	15	13,795,400	0	
Office Equipment	165 items	6	1,883,900	33	465,740
Total items	217 items a)	b)		g)	

AUDITOR CONCLUSION:
NOTE TO STUDENTS: If you believe that the number of items tested is inadequate, state the minimum additional amount to be tested in your conclusion. You should assume that RP will do the additional testing.

Proli Footwear
Repairs and Maintenance Analysis
December 31, 2014

Date	Amount
01/31/12	$31,250
02/28/12	31,250
03/31/12	89,950
04/30/12	39,250
05/31/12	257,960
06/30/12	158,700
07/31/12	109,880
08/31/12	65,400
09/30/12	31,250
10/31/12	48,970
11/30/12	31,604
12/31/12	35,000
Balance per trial balance	$930,464

Audit adjustments:

Balance per audit

Analysis of entries:

Janitorial service: ($8,250/month)	See note	$90,750
Trash removal service: (23,000/month)	See note	253,000
Paint president's office		8,000
Purchase and install new X machine on production line		453,000
Repairs to roof		8,000
Repair rain damaged offices		35,800
Plumbing repairs		11,200
Computer repairs		17,014
Misc: none over $500		53,700
Total		$930,464

Note: This represents only 11 months expense. RP

Proli Footwear
Analysis of Long-Lived Asset Disposals and Related Gains/Losses
December 31, 2014

Description of Item	Cost	Accumulated Depreciation	Book Value	Cash Received *	Gain/ (Loss)
Balance per trial balance					0
Audit adjustments:					
Sale of 1 type E machine – Manufacturing Equipment					
Note: purchased in 1996-15 year life	103,330	103,330	0	12,000	
Sale of 2 type BB equipment – Warehouse Equipment					
Note: purchased in 2001-15 year life	794,960	688,961	105,999	1,000	
Balance per audit	898,290	792,291			

*Since Miscellaneous income (account #8500) was credited for the cash received, an adjusting entry will be required to record the gain or loss on the sale of the assets and the removal of the assets from the books. RP

Proli Footwear
AJE Control-Property, Plant, and Equipment
December 31, 2014

AJE Number	Reference	Accounts/Description	Account Number	Debit	Credit

x = account has impact on income before taxes amount
Impact on income before taxes =   DR/CR

Proli Footwear
Red Flag Events-Property, Plant, and Equipment
December 31, 2014

Event Number	Reference	Auditor Observation

Proli Footwear
Management Letter Comments-Property, Plant, and Equipment
December 31, 2014

Comment Number	Reference	Auditor Observation/ Recommendation	Benefit to Client

Proli Footwear
Time Control
December 31, 2014

Section	Budgeted Time	Time Spent Working with Team	Time Spent Working Alone
6A. Property, Plant, and Equipment	5 hours		

Team member names:

ASSIGNMENT #6B – INTANGIBLE ASSETS

ASSIGNMENT

1. Complete each step of the intangible assets audit program. Indicate completion for each step by making sure that the step is initialed, dated, and that the workpaper reference is indicated. For those audit program steps that are already initialed as having been completed, enter an appropriate date and workpaper reference next to the initials.

2. Be sure to use the appropriate tickmarks to indicate the specific work performed on each piece of audit documentation.

3. Complete and submit for grading all the audit documentation for this section should be organized in the following sequence:
    a. Audit program with dates, initials and audit documentation references;
    b. Completed Lead Schedule with workpaper references, tickmarks indicating work done and appropriate sign-offs;
    c. Specific audit workpaper schedules in sequence with workpaper references, as appropriate, tickmarks indicating work done and appropriate sign-offs;
    d. Adjusting Journal Entry Control containing the proposed AJEs;
    e. Red Flag Events;
    f. Management Letter Comments containing recommended improvements to internal control and other operating issues;
    g. Updated Time Control Worksheet; and
    h. Updated Working Trial Balance (WTB).

4. Each adjusting entry should be entered on the following audit documentation:
    a. Appropriate workpaper schedule
    b. Lead schedule
    c. AJE control
    d. Working trial balance

AUDIT PROGRAM – INTANGIBLE ASSETS

Procedures	Initials	Date	W/P Ref
General			
1. Foot and crossfoot lead schedule and all other PBC schedules			
2. Compare balances on other PBC schedules with balances on lead schedule.			
3. Compare balances on lead schedules with account balances in the trial balance.			
4. Understand client posting regarding amortization in year of acquisition and disposition.			

Procedures	Initials	Date	W/P Ref

Analytical Review

1. Review general ledger accounts, noting any unusual entries. — RP 2/15

2. Review minutes for authorization for acquisitions and disposals, if appropriate. — RP 2/15 DB-2,3,4

Substantive Procedures

1. Recompute/complete amortization expense schedule for the current and all prior years.

2. Compare acquisitions and dispositions with underlying documentation, noting differences, if any. Trace such transactions to cash disbursements and cash receipts. — RP

HELPFUL HINTS FROM THE IN-CHARGE ACCOUNTANT:

1. Use a tickmark to show each work procedure performed.

2. Remember to post adjusting entries affecting the intangible assets section from the previous sections to the intangible assets lead sheet.

3. Be alert for "Red Flag" events. A red flag event is an event or transaction that might indicate fraudulent activity, but needs further investigation to determine:
   a. Whether it was intentional or just human error and
   b. The impact of the event.

4. Refer to an accounting text to refresh your memory about accounting for the impairment of intangibles.

5. Remember that any work RP has completed need not be repeated by you. You may assume that RP has done <u>all</u> the necessary work to complete the work program step correctly. *All of RP's work looks like this.*

Proli Footwear
Lead Schedule - Long-Lived Assets - Intangible Assets
December 31, 2014

Account #	Account Title	Balance per T/B Debit	Balance per T/B Credit	Adjustments Debit	Adjustments Credit	Balance per Audit Debit	Balance per Audit Credit
1540	Trademarks	10,129,800					
1542	Patents	1,328,400					
1545	Goodwill	8,267,700					
Accumulated Amortization:							
1550	Trademarks		1,463,026				
1552	Patents		929,608				
1555	Goodwill		2,765,639				
Amortization Expense:							
7230	Trademarks	253,108					
7232	Patents	47,356					
7235	Goodwill	859,093					
Other Accounts:							
7900	Impairment Loss	0					

Impact of AJEs for this assignment on client's net income before income taxes = _____ DR/CR

110

©Proctor and Poli

Proli Footwear
Amortization Schedule - Trademarks (Indefinite Life Intangibles – Other Than Goodwill)
December 31, 2014

Trademarks: PER BOOKS

Description	Year Acquired	Cost	Accumulated Amortization 12/31/2013	Carrying Value 12/31/2013	Expense 2014	Accumulated Amortization 12/31/2014	Carrying Value 12/31/2014
Dapper®	2010	2,252,700	197,111	2,055,589	56,318	253,429	1,999,271
Leatherworker®	1945	3,000	3,000	0	0	3,000	0
Litetech®	1980	5,000	4,188	812	125	4,313	687
Mudhoppers®	2012	2,641,800	99,068	2,542,732	66,045	165,113	2,476,687
Proli®	1941	2,500	2,500	0	0	2,500	0
Sportech®	2001	2,795,800	873,688	1,922,112	69,895	943,583	1,852,217
Woodland®	2013	2,429,000	30,363	2,398,637	60,725	91,088	2,337,912
Subtotal Trademarks		10,129,800	1,209,918	8,919,882	253,108	1,463,026	8,666,774

Trademarks: PER AUDITORS

Description	Year Acquired	<<<<Fair Value Test>>>> Adjusted Carrying Value 1/1/2014	Fair Value 12/31/2014	Impairment Loss Yes/No	Calculated Impairment Loss Amount
Dapper®	2010 M	2,055,589			
Leatherworker®	1945 D	0			
Litetech®	1980 M	812			
Mudhoppers®	2012 M	2,542,732			
Proli®	1941 D	0			
Sportech®	2001 M	1,922,112			
Woodland®	2013 M	2,398,637			
Subtotal Trademarks					

Note: The amortization method used by the client for trademarks is straight-line over 40 years.

Trademarks are classified as indefinite life intangibles and require an annual fair value test to determine the lack or presence of impairment. Therefore, the amortization expense for 2014 needs to be reversed to properly show the carrying value of the trademarks as of January 1, 2014. RP

The following trademarks were internally generated: Leatherworker and Proli; all other trademarks were acquired when Proli purchased other companies.

D = Traced registration and legal fees to the cash disbursements journal.
M = Traced the authorization to purchase the company and the purchase price to the Board of Directors' minutes.

AJE 6B-1
Accumulated Amortization   253,108   253,108
Amortization Expense   253,108

©Proctor and Poli

Proli Footwear
Amortization Schedule - Patents (Limited Life Intangibles)
December 31, 2014

Patents: PER BOOKS

Description	Year Acquired	Cost	Accumulated Amortization 12/31/2013	Carrying Value 12/31/2013	Expense 2014	Accumulated Amortization 12/31/2014	Carrying Value 12/31/2014
Patent #2698	1950 M	381,280	381,280	0	0	381,280	0
Patent #6974	1999 M	609,500	441,888	167,612	30,475	472,363	137,137
Patent #9767	2010 M	337,620	59,084	278,536	16,881	75,965	261,655
Subtotal Patents		1,328,400	882,252	446,148	47,356	929,608	398,792

Patents: PER AUDITORS

Description	Year Acquired	<<<<<Recoverability Test>>>>> Adjusted Carrying Value 1/1/2014	Expected Future Cash Flow Undiscounted	Impairment Loss Yes/No	Fair Value Test Fair Value	Calculated Impairment Loss Amount
Patent #2698	1950 M	0				
Patent #6974	1999 M	167,612	357,260			
Patent #9767	2010 M	278,536	119,460			
Subtotal Patents						

Note: The amortization method used by the client for patents is straight-line over 20 years.

Patents are considered limited life intangibles that require the use of both the recoverability test and the fair value test. Therefore, the amortization expense for 2014 needs to be reversed to properly show the carrying value (i.e. book value) of the patents as of January 1, 2014. In addition, the client has calculated the undiscounted expected future cash flow for the two patents that are still under patent protection. RP

AJE 6B-2

Accumulated Amortization   47,356
    Amortization Expense   47,356

M = Traced the authorization to purchase the patent and the purchase price to the Board of Directors' minutes.

Proli Footwear
Amortization Schedule - Goodwill (Indefinite Life Intangibles)
December 31, 2014

Goodwill: PER BOOKS

Description	Year Acquired	Cost	Accumulated Amortization 12/31/13	Carrying Value 12/31/13	Expense 2014	Amortization 12/31/14	Carrying Value 12/31/14
Purchase of Dapper Manufacturing Co.	2001	2,438,000	761,875	1,676,125	60,950	822,825	1,615,175
Purchase of Softshoe, Inc.	2012	3,728,000	1,118,400	2,609,600	745,600	1,864,000	1,864,000
Purchase of Woodland	2013	2,101,700	26,271	2,075,429	52,543	78,814	2,022,886
Subtotal Goodwill		8,267,700	1,906,546	6,361,154	859,093	2,765,639	5,502,061

Goodwill: PER AUDITORS

Description	Year Acquired	Adjusted Carrying Value 1/1/2014	Net Identifiable Assets, Excluding Goodwill	Fair Value Reporting Unit Test Net Assets Including Goodwill	Fair Value	Impairment Loss Yes/No	Fair Value Test of Goodwill Implied Fair Value of Goodwill	Calculated Impairment Loss Amount
Purchase of Dapper Manufacturing Co.	2001 M	1,676,125	6,343,200					
Purchase of Softshoe, Inc.	2012 M	2,609,600	9,002,700					
Purchase of Woodland	2013 M	2,075,429	5,172,000					
Subtotal Goodwill		6,361,154	20,517,900					

Note: The amortization method used by the client for Goodwill is straight-line over 40 years for Dapper and Woodland and straight-line over 5 years for Softshoe.

Goodwill is subject to the impairment test using a two-step process. The fair value test is applied first to the reporting unit and then to the goodwill. Therefore, the amortization expense for 2014 needs to be reversed to properly show the carrying value (i.e. book value) of the goodwill as of January 1, 2014.   RP

AJE 6B-3

Accumulated Amortization	859,093	859,093

M = Traced the authorization to purchase the company and the purchase price to the Board of Directors' minutes

113

©Proctor and Poli

TURKEY BAY VALUATIONS, LLC
2 CANDLEWEED AVENUE
TURKEY BAY, CT

January 25, 2015

Ms. Patricia Fair
West and Fair, CPAs, LLC
Stamford, CT

Dear Ms. Fair:

The enclosed valuation report has been developed for the exclusive and confidential use of West and Fair, CPAs, LLC and this report has been prepared under the direct supervision of the undersigned. The purpose of the valuation is to render an estimate of the fair value of patents, trademarks, and goodwill of Proli Footwear as of December 31, 2014. This valuation is to be used in determining the impairment of these intangible assets.

Based upon our study and review procedures, we have concluded that the fair values of these intangible assets are as follows:

Intangible Asset	Fair Value
Trademarks:	
Dapper®	912,400
Litetech®	389,800
Mudhoppers®	1,194,600
Sportech®	1,768,900
Woodland®	2,790,000
Patents:	
Patent #6974	107,500
Patent #9767	212,240
Goodwill related to purchase of:	
Sportech Co.	7,415,000
Softshoe, Inc.	13,675,000
Woodland Corporation	8,535,000

In preparing our report, we have relied on historical financial information provided to us. This financial information has not been audited or reviewed by us and we do not express an opinion or any form of assurance on this financial information. The accompanying report discusses all the assumptions and limiting conditions that apply to this opinion of value and are integral to the understanding of the opinion.

This engagement was not contingent upon developing or reporting predetermined results. Our compensation for completing this assignment is not contingent upon the development or reporting of a predetermined value or direction in value that favors the cause of the client, the amount of the value opinion, the attainment of a stipulated result, or the occurrence of a subsequent event directly related to the intended use of this appraisal.

We have performed a valuation engagement and present our report in conformity with valuation standards of the American Institute of Certified Public Accountants (AICPA) and National Association of Certified Valuation Analysts (NACVA). These standards define a valuation engagement as "an engagement to estimate value in which a valuation analyst determines an estimate of the value of a subject interest by performing appropriate procedures, as outlined in the Standards for Valuation Services, and is free to apply the valuation approaches and methods he or she deems appropriate in the circumstances. The valuation analyst expresses the results of the valuation engagement as a conclusion of value, which may be either a single amount or a range."

No one provided significant business appraisal assistance in preparing this report other than the person signing the certification.

Sincerely yours,

Turkey Bay Valuations, LLC

Hees Worthit
_____
By: Hees Worthit, CPA/ABV/CFF, CVA

Proli Footwear
Amortization Policy
December 31, 2014

Account Title	Method	Useful Life	Salvage Value
Trademarks	Straight-line	40 years	0
Patents	Straight-line	20 years	0
Goodwill:			
Sportech Co.	Straight-line	40 years	N/A
Softshoe, Inc.	Straight-line	5 years	N/A
Woodland Corporation	Straight-line	40 years	N/A

Note 1: Per the client's policy and procedures manual, in the year of acquisition and disposal, 1/2 year amortization is taken. RP

Note 2: Book and tax bases are the same for all buildings, leased buildings, and equipment (i.e. book depreciation = tax depreciation). acquired before 8/11/93 is still not deductible for tax purposes. RP

Proli Footwear
AJE Control-Intangible Assets
December 31, 2014

AJE Number	Reference	Accounts/Description	Account Number	Debit	Credit

x = account has impact on income before taxes amount

Impact on income before taxes =   DR/CR

Proli Footwear
Red Flag Events-Intangible Assets
December 31, 2014

Event Number	Reference	Auditor Observation

Proli Footwear
Management Letter Comments-Intangible Assets
December 31, 2014

Comment Number	Reference	Auditor Observation/ Recommendation	Benefit to Client

Proli Footwear
Time Control
December 31, 2014

Section	Budgeted Time	Time Spent Working with Team	Time Spent Working Alone
6B. Intangible Assets	4 hours		

Team member names:

ASSIGNMENT #7A – CURRENT LIABILITIES

ASSIGNMENT

1. Complete each step of the current liabilities audit program. Indicate completion for each step by making sure that the step is initialed, dated, and that the workpaper reference is indicated. For those audit program steps that are already initialed as having been completed, enter an appropriate date and workpaper reference next to the initials.

2. Be sure to use the appropriate tickmarks to indicate the specific work performed on each piece of audit documentation.

3. Complete and submit for grading all the audit documentation for this section organized in the following sequence:
   a. Audit program with dates, initials and audit documentation references;
   b. Completed Lead Schedule with workpaper references, tickmarks indicating work done and appropriate sign-offs;
   c. Specific audit workpaper schedules in sequence with workpaper references, as appropriate, tickmarks indicating work done and appropriate sign-offs;
   d. Adjusting Journal Entry Control containing the proposed AJEs;
   e. Red Flag Events;
   f. Management Letter Comments containing recommended improvements to internal control and other operating issues;
   g. Updated Time Control Worksheet; and
   h. Updated Working Trial Balance (WTB).

4. Each adjusting entry should be entered on the following audit documentation:
   a. Appropriate workpaper schedule
   b. Lead schedule
   c. AJE control
   d. Working trial balance

AUDIT PROGRAM – CURRENT LIABILITIES

Procedures	Initials	Date	W/P Ref
General			
1. Foot and crossfoot lead schedule and all other PBC schedules.			
2. Compare balances on other PBC schedules with balances on the lead schedules.			
3. Compare balances on lead schedule with account balances in the trial balance.			

Procedures	Initials	Date	W/P Ref

Analytical Review Procedures

1. Review entries to liability and related accounts for the period and investigate large or unusual items. — RP

2. Review minutes for authorization for:

    a. Bonus payments — RP — 2/15 — EA-6

    b. Borrowings — RP — 2/15 — EA-3

Substantive Audit Procedures

Accrued Expenses

1. Examine supporting documentation. — RP

2. Review January check register for unrecorded December liabilities for the Proli, CT facilities.

3. Review January check register for unrecorded December liabilities for the Walton, FL facilities.

4. Review January check register for unrecorded December liabilities for the Waterbury, CT facilities.

5. Trace bonus payments during the year to payroll cash payments journal. — RP

6. Recalculate bonuses payable.

7. Recalculate commissions payable.

8. Prepare adjusting journal entries, if necessary.

Notes Payable (current)

9. Review clerical accuracy of carrying value of notes payable.

10. Compare amount confirmed by bank with audit documentation and lead schedule.

11. Review for proper financial statement classification and disclosure.

Other Items

12. Recalculate bonus expense.

13. Commissions expense:

    a. On a test basis, trace information from sales rep order documentation to sales rep commission list. — RP

    b. On a test basis, vouch information from the sales rep commission list to sales rep order documentation. — RP

    c. Recalculate commissions expense.

14. Recalculate rent expense

HELPFUL HINTS FROM THE IN-CHARGE ACCOUNTANT:

1. Use a tickmark to show each work procedure performed.

2. Remember to post adjusting entries affecting current liabilities from previous sections to the current liabilities lead sheet.

3. Be alert for "Red Flag" events. A red flag event is an event or transaction that might indicate fraudulent activity, but needs further investigation to determine:
   a. Whether it was intentional or just human error and
   b. The impact of the event.

4. Remember that any work RP has completed need not be repeated by you. You may assume that RP has done all the necessary work to complete the work program step correctly. *All of RP's work looks like this.*

Proli Footwear
Lead Schedule - Current Liabilities
December 31, 2014

Account Number	Account Title	Balance per T/B Debit	Balance per T/B Credit	Adjustments Debit	Adjustments Credit	Balance per Audit Debit	Balance per Audit Credit
2200	Note Payable		12,800,000				
2400	Accrued Expenses		7,769,300				
2410	Interest Payable-Note Payable	0	0				
	Related Accounts:						
7440	Commissions Expense	1,370,007					
7460	Bonus Expense	100,000					
7470	Warranty Expense	292,000					
8310	Interest Expense-Note Payable	1,181,006					

Impact of AJEs for this assignment on net income before income taxes = _____ DR/CR

Proli Footwear
Accrued Expenses
December 31, 2014

Vendor		Amount
Proli, CT facilities:		
Big City Office Supply		124,380
Blue Star Restaurant		1,175
Bonuses Payable	1)	400,000
Commissions Payable		87,000
Connecticut Electric - Proli facilities		75,450
Conn Phone - Proli facilities		192,150
Lucky Advertising	2)	357,000
P&P Mobile Phone		25,600
Payroll taxes-federal-due Jan 15		87,254
Payroll taxes-state-due Jan 15		19,720
Proli Accounting Temps		35,800
Proli Electric		63,800
Proli Florist		27,890
Proli Insurance Agency		788,900
Proli Propane		66,600
Proli Water Company		136,780
Salaries Payable	3)	148,600
Thumpem, Lumpem & Howe		130,000
Warranty Payable		424,000
Workers' compensation insurance agency		731,500
Misc: None over $5,000		3,421,011
Subtotal Proli, CT facilities		7,344,610

1) Salary expense was debited when client recorded this accrual RP
2) The Executive V-P of Lucky Advertising is Robbert Baddude, the brother of Brian Baddude. Is there a conflict of interest or related party issue? RP
3) The payroll accrual recorded on the books by client on 12/31/14 was:

Salary Expense	48,600	
Bonus Expense	100,000	
Accrued Expenses		148,600

Proli Footwear
Accrued Expenses (continued)
December 31, 2014

Vendor	Amount
Subtotal Proli, CT facilities	7,344,610
Walton, FL facilities:	
Fred's Cleaning Service	8,250
Subtotal Walton, FL facilities	8,250
Waterbury, CT facilities:	
Conn Phone - Waterbury facilities	187,680
Connecticut Electric - Waterbury facilities	23,500
Waterbury Gas	38,950
Waterbury Trash Service	7,890
Waterbury Water	158,420
Subtotal Waterbury, CT facilities	416,440
Balance per trial balance	7,769,300
Audit adjustments:	

Balance per audit:

Proli Footwear
Interest Expense and Payable Analysis – Note Payable
December 31, 2014

	Balance per Client	Balance per Audit	Adjustment Required
Interest Expense Calculation:			
Amount Borrowed	12,800,000 M		
Interest Rate			
Date of Loan		3/1/2014 L	
Interest Expense			
Interest Payable Calculation:			
Interest Payable			
Audit Adjustment per above			
Interest Payable			

Note: Principal repayment due on due date; interest payments are made quarterly   RP
L=Per loan agreement
M=Traced authorization to the Board of Directors' minutes.

PROLI FOOTWEAR
STAMFORD, CONNECTICUT

January 5, 2015

Walton Trust
Walton, FL

Dear Sirs:

Our independent auditors, West & Fair CPAs, LLC, are performing an audit of our financial statements. We have provided our accountants with information regarding deposit and loan balances as of **December 31, 2014**. Please confirm the accuracy of this information, noting any discrepancies in the information provided. If other balances are outstanding, please include that information. Please return this letter directly to our accountants: **West & Fair CPAs, LLC; Stamford, CT**

1. Deposit information

Account Name	Account No.	Interest Rate	Balance
None			

2. Loan information

Account No. Description	Balance	Monthly Payment	Date Due	Interest Rate	Date through Which Interest Is Paid	Description of Collateral
Mortgage #2	883,458	11,402.02		14%	12/1/2014	Land & Buildings - Walton, FL
Mortgage #3	641,702	6,237.62		11%	12/1/2014	
Note Payable	12,800,000	N/A	3/1/2016	11%	12/31/2014	None

Very truly yours,
Harold F. Heele,
Harold F. Heele,
Vice President – Finance and Chief Financial Officer

CONFIRMATION: The information presented above is in agreement with our records. Although we have not performed a detailed search of our records, no other deposit or loan accounts have come to our attention except as noted below.

Exceptions or Comments:
...None...

Mary Jones	_January 14, 2015_	_Bank Manager_	
(Institution's Authorized Signature)	(Date)	(Title)	

Proli Footwear
Commissions Expense and Payable Analysis
December 31, 2014

	Balance per Client	Balance per Audit	Adjustment Required
Commissions Expense Calculation:			
Gross Sales			
Sales made by sales reps = 32.3% of Gross Sales	1)		C
Commission Rate	2)	3%	
Commissions Expense			
Commissions Payable Calculation:			
Accrued Expenses-Commissions Payable			
Audit Adjustment per above			
Accrued Expenses-Commissions Payable			

1) Per the Sales Manager, 32.3% of gross sales are made by independent sales reps.
2) Per the Sales Manager, independent sales reps are paid commissions of 3% of gross sales. RP

C = Compared list of sales made by sales reps which approximates 32.3%   RP
On a test basis, I traced information from sales order documentation to the sales rep commissions list. RP
On a test basis, I vouched information from the sales rep commissions list to the sales rep order documentation.   RP

Proli Footwear
Bonus Expense and Payable Analysis
December 31, 2014

	Balance per Client	Balance per Audit	Adjustment Required
Bonus Expense Calculation:			
Net Sales for year		a)	
Cost of Goods Sold for year		b)	
Gross Profit for year			
Bonus rate = 1.8% of Gross Profit M			
Bonus Expense	100,000 T		c)
Bonus Payable Calculation:			
Accrued Expense-Bonus Payable 400,000		c)	

Gross Sales per Client	148,235,225 TB	
AJE from Cash Section	-28,900	
AJES from Accounts Receivable Section	-670,499	
Adjusted Gross Sales		147,535,826
Sales Discounts		0 TB
Sales Returns/Allowances	1,117,535 TB	
AJES from Accounts Receivable section	44,926	
Adjusted Sales Returns/Allowances		1,162,461
Net Sales		146,373,365 a)
Cost of Goods Sold per Client	108,711,900 TB	
AJES from Inventory section	-591,563	
Net Cost Of Goods Sold		108,120,337 b)

Note: Per client, $400,000 of bonus expense was recorded in salaries expense (account #7450)
RP

M = Examined minutes of Board of Directors meeting on 12/1/2014 noting authorization for a bonus of 1.8% of gross profit to be divided among senior management of the company. RP
T = Traced to cash disbursements journal for payroll cash account. RP

AUDIT MEMO
West & Fair CPAs, LLC
Stamford, CT

Re: Proli Footwear - Warranty Expense

Proli provides a limited warranty for the replacement of defective products sold within the 12 month period after sale. The Company estimates the costs that may be incurred under its limited warranty and records a liability in the amount of such costs at the time product revenue is recognized. Factors that affect the Company's warranty liability include the sales level and the historical and anticipated future rates of warranty claims. Accruals for product warranties are included in accrued expenses in the accompanying Balance Sheet. Changes in the accrued warranty account for the years ended December 31, 2014 and 2013 are summarized in the following chart:

Accrued Expenses-Warranty Payable	2014	2013
Beginning Balance	431,000	578,000
Year End Expense Accrual	292,000	280,000
Actual Warranty Costs Incurred on prior year sales	(299,000)	(427,000)
Ending Balance	424,000	431,000

As a result of my review and analysis of the warranty liability account and the related expense[a], the following was determined:

- Additions to the liability account and the related expense are being accrued at a rate of approximately 0.2% of Net Sales in 2014 and 2013. Controller Baddude says this reflects Proli's historical experience over the last 10 years.

- An analysis by audit staff member, Fred Gogetter, indicates that actual warranty costs recognized since 2004 are approximately 0.3% of annual net sales.

- It has been determined that some warranty costs incurred by Proli for 2014 were erroneously debited to the Other Assets account rather than the liability account. The amount of this error is $102,000.

Further discussions with Controller Baddude indicated that Proli management believes that the rate of 0.2% of net sales is a reasonable estimate of warranty expense and reflects Proli's expected future liability in this category. Therefore Proli Management feels that no change in the accrual is warranted.

After discussion with Partner Patricia Fair it was decided that an adjustment is necessary to increase the warranty liability to reflect the 0.3% accrual rate. See EA-9 for this calculation.

[a]Note to students: These analyses are not included in this book.

Proli Footwear
Warranty Expense and Payable Analysis
December 31, 2014

	Balance per Client	Balance per Audit	Adjustment Required
Warranty Expense Calculation:			
Net Sales		a)	
Warranty Expense Rate		b)	
Warranty Expense		c)=a)*b)	
Warranty Payable Calculation:			
Accrued Expenses-Warranty Payable	d)		
Audit Adjustment per above	d)		
	d)		
Accrued Expenses-Warranty Payable		Σd)	

Proli Footwear
AJE Control-Current Liabilities
December 31, 2014

AJE Number	Reference	Accounts/Description	Account Number	Debit	Credit

x = account has impact on income before taxes amount

Impact on income before taxes =   DR/CR

Proli Footwear
Red Flag Events-Current Liabilities
December 31, 2014

Event Number	Reference	Auditor Observation

Proli Footwear
Management Letter Comments-Current Liabilities
December 31, 2014

Comment Number	Reference	Auditor Observation/ Recommendation	Benefit to Client

Proli Footwear
Time Control
December 31, 2014

Section	Budgeted Time	Time Spent Working with Team	Time Spent Working Alone
7A. Current Liabilities	4 hours		

Team member names:

ASSIGNMENT #7B – LEASE LIABILITIES

ASSIGNMENT

1. Complete each step of the lease liabilities audit program. Indicate completion for each step by making sure that the step is initialed, dated, and that the workpaper reference is indicated. For those audit program steps that are already initialed as having been completed, enter an appropriate date and workpaper reference next to the initials.

2. Be sure to use the appropriate tickmarks to indicate the specific work performed on each piece of audit documentation.

3. Complete and submit for grading all the audit documentation for this section organized in the following sequence:
   a. Audit program with dates, initials and audit documentation references;
   b. Completed Lead Schedule with workpaper references, tickmarks indicating work done and appropriate sign-offs;
   c. Specific audit workpaper schedules in sequence with workpaper references, as appropriate, tickmarks indicating work done and appropriate sign-offs;
   d. Adjusting Journal Entry Control containing the proposed AJEs;
   e. Red Flag Events;
   f. Management Letter Comments containing recommended improvements to internal control and other operating issues;
   g. Updated Time Control Worksheet; and
   h. Updated Working Trial Balance (WTB).

4. Each adjusting entry should be entered on the following audit documentation:
   a. Appropriate workpaper schedule
   b. Lead schedule
   c. AJE control
   d. Working trial balance

AUDIT PROGRAM – LEASE LIABILITIES

Procedures	Initials	Date	W/P Ref
General			
1. Foot and crossfoot lead schedule and all other PBC schedules.			
2. Compare balances on other PBC schedules with balances on the lead schedules.			
3. Compare balances on lead schedule with account balances in the trial balance.			

Procedures	Initials	Date	W/P Ref

Analytical Review Procedures

1. Review entries to liability and related accounts for the period and investigate large or unusual items. RP

2. Review entries to related interest expense accounts. RP

3. Review minutes for authorization for lease agreements RP 2/15 EB2-EB-7

Substantive Audit Procedures

1. Confirm leases. RP

2. Examine supporting documentation. RP

3. Recalculate current portion of lease obligations.

4. Review clerical accuracy of carrying value of long-term lease obligations.

5. Compare amount confirmed with audit documentation and lead schedule. RP 2/15 (not included)

6. Review for proper financial statement classification and disclosure.

7. Recalculate rent expense

8. Recalculate interest expense. RP 2/15

9. Prepare adjusting journal entries, if necessary.

HELPFUL HINTS FROM THE IN-CHARGE ACCOUNTANT:

1. Use a tickmark to show each work procedure performed.

2. Remember to post adjusting entries affecting lease liabilities from previous sections to the lease liabilities lead sheet.

3. Be alert for "Red Flag" events. A red flag event is an event or transaction that might indicate fraudulent activity, but needs further investigation to determine:
   a. Whether it was intentional or just human error and
   b. The impact of the event.

4. Refer to an accounting text and review the rules related to classify leases as capital or operating leases. All debt amortization schedules are based on the annuity due concept of amortization. Please refer to a textbook to refresh your understanding of annuity due versus annuity in advance.

5. Refer to an accounting text and read about prior period adjustments. Remember that prior period adjustments occur when income statement/retained earning adjustments are proposed after the books have been closed. Remember to include income tax effects, if appropriate. All deferred tax liabilities and assets should be recorded in Account # 2700. The Company's combined federal and state income tax rate is 40%.

6. Remember that any work RP has completed need not be repeated by you. You may assume that RP has done all the necessary work to complete the work program step correctly. All of RP's work looks like this.

Proli Footwear
Lead Schedule - Lease Liabilities
December 31, 2014

Account Number	Account Title	Balance per T/B Debit	Balance per T/B Credit	Adjustments Debit	Adjustments Credit	Balance per Audit Debit	Balance per Audit Credit
Current Maturities of Leases							
	Lease L1		15,064				
	Lease L2A		119,622				
	Lease L2B		0				
	Lease L3		0				
	Lease L4		194,039				
	Lease L5		74,398				
2110	Total Current Maturities		403,123				

139

Proli Footwear
Lead Schedule - Lease Liabilities
December 31, 2014

Account Number	Account Title	Balance per T/B Debit	Balance per T/B Credit	Adjustments Debit	Adjustments Credit	Balance per Audit Debit	Balance per Audit Credit
	Long-Term Portion of Leases						
	Lease L1		926,079				
	Lease L2A		163,602				
	Lease L2B		0				
	Lease L3		0				
	Lease L4		0				
	Lease L5		206,770				
2510	Total Long-Term Portion		1,296,451				
	Related Accounts						
2411	Interest Payable-Leases		0				
7350	Rent Expense	1,222,480					
8320	Interest Expense-Leases	217,577					

Impact of AJEs for this assignment on net income before income taxes =   DR/CR

140

Note to Student: Please note that RP has examined the lease agreements and verified the appropriate information. RP has also recomputed and verified all interest and rent expense amounts. If you determine that the client has improperly classified any of the leases the following accounts will need to be adjusted:

- Leased asset: record or remove from books
- Accumulated depreciation: record or remove from books (remember client policy regarding first and last years' depreciation)
- Current maturity of lease: record or remove from books
- Long-term portion of lease: record or remove from books
- Interest payable (accrued expense) for January 1, 2015 payment: record or remove from books
- Interest expense for year 2014: record or remove from books
- Rent expense: record or remove from books
- Prior period adjustment will be the difference – this results from the prior years' interest expense and rent expense that were (or were not) deducted in prior years
- Deferred tax asset/liability must be calculated on the prior period adjustment – remember that the client's tax rate is 40%

Proli Footwear
Lease Classification Test
December 31, 2014

Lease L1: Proli, CT: Principal sales, marketing, and executive offices   MC

Lease Term:	L 2001-2031
Guaranteed Residual Value:	L $150,000
	EB-9
Monthly Rent Payment:	L $11,378 EB-11
Client classification:	Capital

| Test 1: Does ownership transfer to the lessee at end of lease term? | Yes/No | L | NO |

| Test 2: Is there a bargain purchase option? | Yes/No | L | NO |

Test 3: Does the lease term exceed 75% of the life of the asset?   Yes/No   YES

| | Lease Term: | L | 30 | = 86% |
| 1) | Economic life: | | 35 | |

Test 4: Does the present value (PV) of the minimum lease
payments exceed 90% of the fair value of the asset?   Yes/No   NO

| 2) | PV: | L 1,042,810 | = 86% |
| | Fair value of asset: | A 1,215,000 | |

| Proper lease classification based on above tests: | Capital/Operating | Capital |

Auditor Conclusion: Lease is properly/improperly classified by client.   Properly

NOTE from RP: Make one adjustment for each lease; the client's tax rate is 40%

L = Examined lease agreement and agreed information to the lease. Lease does not contain a bargain purchase option or penalties for not renewing the lease.

M = Traced the authorization to enter into the lease agreement to the Board of Directors' minutes. Per the minutes, when the lease was signed, the Company had no intention of retaining ownership at the end of the lease.

A = Traced value to appraisal done at inception of lease.

C = Confirmation received from lessor. Verified all terms of the agreement and noted that lessor confirms that 12/1/2014 lease payment was made. **[Note to student:** Confirmations not included in this book.**]**

1) Based on economic lives of other buildings the company owns. See DA-7.

2) Present value of minimum lease payments calculated at inception of lease = Lease obligation at inception of lease. RP

Proli Footwear
Lease Classification Test
December 31, 2014

Lease L2A: Proli, CT: Main warehouse and distribution facility	MC
Lease Term:	L 2006-2016
Guaranteed Residual Value:	L $100,000
Monthly Rent Payment:	L $11,880
Client classification:	Capital

Test 1: Does ownership transfer to the lessee at end of lease term?	Yes/No	L	NO

Test 2: Is there a bargain purchase option?	Yes/No	L	NO

Test 3: Does the lease term exceed 75% of the life of the asset?   Yes/No

		Lease Term:	L	10	=
1)		Economic life:		35	

Test 4: Does the present value of the minimum lease
payments exceed 90% of the fair value of the asset?   Yes/No

2)	PV:	L 943,406	=
	Fair value of asset:	A 971,000	

Proper lease classification based on above tests:	Capital/Operating

Auditor Conclusion: Lease is properly/improperly classified by client.

NOTE from RP: Make one adjustment for each lease; the client's tax rate is 40%

L = Examined lease agreement and agreed information to the lease. Lease does not contain a bargain purchase option or penalties for not renewing the lease.

M = Traced the authorization to enter into the lease agreement to the Board of Directors' minutes. Per the minutes, when the lease was signed, the Company had no intention of retaining ownership at the end of the lease.

A = Traced value to appraisal done at inception of lease.

C = Confirmation received from lessor. Verified all terms of the agreement and noted that lessor confirms that 12/1/2014 lease payment was made. **[Note to student:** Confirmations not included in this book.**]**

1) Based on economic lives of other buildings the company owns. See DA-7.

2) Present value of minimum lease payments calculated at inception of lease = Lease obligation at inception of lease. RP

Proli Footwear
Lease Classification Test
December 31, 2014

Lease L2B: Proli, CT: Main warehouse and distribution facility	MC
Lease Term:	L year-to-year
Guaranteed Residual Value:	L $0
Monthly Rent Payment:	L $14,000
Client classification:	Operating

Test 1: Does ownership transfer to the lessee at end of lease term?   Yes/No   L   NO

Test 2: Is there a bargain purchase option?   Yes/No   L   NO

Test 3: Does the lease term exceed 75% of the life of the asset?   Yes/No

	Lease Term:	L	1	
1)	Economic life:		35	=

Test 4: Does the present value of the minimum lease
payments exceed 90% of the fair value of the asset?   Yes/No

2)	PV:	L 160,570	
	Fair value of asset:	A 1,450,000	=

Proper lease classification based on above tests: Capital/Operating

Auditor Conclusion: Lease is properly/improperly classified by client.

NOTE from RP: Make one adjustment for each lease; the client's tax rate is 40%

L = Examined lease agreement and agreed information to the lease. Lease does not contain a bargain purchase option or penalties for not renewing the lease.

M = Traced the authorization to enter into the lease agreement to the Board of Directors' minutes. Per the minutes, when the lease was signed, the Company had no intention of retaining ownership at the end of the lease.

A = Traced value to appraisal done at inception of lease.

C = Confirmation received from lessor. Verified all terms of the agreement and noted that lessor confirms that 12/1/2014 lease payment was made. **[Note to student:** Confirmations not included in this book.**]**

1) Based on economic lives of other buildings the company owns. See DA-7.

2) Present value of minimum lease payments calculated at inception of lease = Lease obligation at inception of lease. RP

Proli Footwear
Lease Classification Test
December 31, 2014

Lease L3: Walton, FL: Warehouse and distribution facility   MC

Lease Term:	L 2001-2016
Guaranteed Residual Value:	L $100,000
Monthly Rent Payment:	L $4,540
Client classification:	Operating

Test 1: Does ownership transfer to the lessee at end of lease term?   Yes/No   L   NO

Test 2: Is there a bargain purchase option?   Yes/No   L   NO

Test 3: Does the lease term exceed 75% of the life of the asset?   Yes/No

           Lease Term: L   15   =

   1)   Economic life: 35

Test 4: Does the present value of the minimum lease
payments exceed 90% of the fair value of the asset?   Yes/No

      2)   PV: L 377,089   =

      Fair value of asset: A 400,000

Proper lease classification based on above tests: Capital/Operating

Auditor Conclusion: Lease is properly/improperly classified by client.

NOTE from RP: Make one adjustment for each lease; the client's tax rate is 40%

L = Examined lease agreement and agreed information to the lease. Lease does not contain a bargain purchase option or penalties for not renewing the lease.

M = Traced the authorization to enter into the lease agreement to the Board of Directors' minutes. Per the minutes, when the lease was signed, the Company had no intention of retaining ownership at the end of the lease.

A = Traced value to appraisal done at inception of lease.

C = Confirmation received from lessor. Verified all terms of the agreement and noted that lessor confirms that 12/1/2014 lease payment was made. **[Note to student:** Confirmations not included in this book.**]**

1) Based on economic lives of other buildings the company owns. See DA-7.

2) Present value of minimum lease payments calculated at inception of lease = Lease obligation at inception of lease. RP

Proli Footwear
Lease Classification Test
December 31, 2014

Lease L4: Walton, FL: Warehouse and distribution facility   MC

Lease Term:	L 2001-2015
Guaranteed Residual Value:	L $150,000
Monthly Rent Payment:	L $13,330
Client classification:	Capital

Test 1: Does ownership transfer to the lessee at end of lease term?   Yes/No   L   NO

Test 2: Is there a bargain purchase option?   Yes/No   L   NO

Test 3: Does the lease term exceed 75% of the life of the asset?   Yes/No

       Lease Term: L   <u>14</u>   =

   1)   Economic life: 35

Test 4: Does the present value of the minimum lease
payments exceed 90% of the fair value of the asset?   Yes/No

      2)   **PV:**   L <u>1,064,826</u> =

     Fair value of asset: A 1,074,000

Proper lease classification based on above tests: Capital/Operating

Auditor Conclusion: Lease is properly/improperly classified by client.

NOTE from RP: Make one adjustment for each lease; the client's tax rate is 40%

L = Examined lease agreement and agreed information to the lease. Lease does not contain a bargain purchase option or penalties for not renewing the lease.

M = Traced the authorization to enter into the lease agreement to the Board of Directors' minutes. Per the minutes, when the lease was signed, the Company had no intention of retaining ownership at the end of the lease.

A = Traced value to appraisal done at inception of lease.

C = Confirmation received from lessor. Verified all terms of the agreement and noted that lessor confirms that 12/1/2014 lease payment was made. **[Note to student:** Confirmations not included in this book.**]**

1) Based on economic lives of other buildings the company owns. See DA-7.

2) Present value of minimum lease payments calculated at inception of lease = Lease obligation at inception of lease. RP

Proli Footwear
Lease Classification Test
December 31, 2014

Lease L5: Waterbury, CT: Manufacturing, warehousing and offices for Mudhoppers, Inc. *MC*

Lease Term:	*L 2012-2017*
Guaranteed Residual Value:	*L $75,000*
Monthly Rent Payment:	*L $8,057*
Client classification:	*Capital*

Test 1: Does ownership transfer to the lessee at end of lease term? Yes/No *L   NO*

Test 2: Is there a bargain purchase option? Yes/No *L   NO*

Test 3: Does the lease term exceed 75% of the life of the asset? Yes/No

	Lease Term:	*L 5*	*=*
1)	Economic life:	*35*	

Test 4: Does the present value of the minimum lease
payments exceed 90% of the fair value of the asset? Yes/No

	PV:	*L 438,946*	*=*
2)	Fair value of asset:	*A 450,000*	

Proper lease classification based on above tests:

Auditor Conclusion: Lease is properly/improperly classified by client.

NOTE from RP: Make one adjustment for each lease; the client's tax rate is 40%

L = Examined lease agreement and agreed information to the lease. Lease does not contain a bargain purchase option or penalties for not renewing the lease.

M = Traced the authorization to enter into the lease agreement to the Board of Directors' minutes. Per the minutes, when the lease was signed, the Company had no intention of retaining ownership at the end of the lease.

A = Traced value to appraisal done at inception of lease.

C = Confirmation received from lessor. Verified all terms of the agreement and noted that lessor confirms that 12/1/2014 lease payment was made. **[Note to student: Confirmations not included in this book.]**

1) Based on economic lives of other buildings the company owns. See DA-7.

2) Present value of minimum lease payments calculated at inception of lease = Lease obligation at inception of lease. RP

　　　　　　　　　　147

Proli Footwear
Interest Information
December 31, 2014

Year		Incremental Borrowing Rates
2001	R	13%
2006	R	10%
2012	R	9%
2014	R	10%

R = Verified calculation by
recomputation and referencing prior
year financial statements.   RP

Proli Footwear
Rent Expense Analysis
December 31, 2014

Lease ID	Monthly Lease Payment	Lease Classification per Client	Rent Expense per Books	Lease Classification per Audit
L1	11,378	Capital	0	
L2A	11,880	Capital	0	
L2B	14,000	Operating	168,000	
L3	4,540	Operating	54,480	
L4	13,330	Capital	0	
L5	8,057	Capital	0	
Rented advertising space on Internet 1)			1,000,000	
Balance per trial balance			1,222,480	

Audit adjustments

Balance per audit

1) Amount paid to Lucky Advertising in November 2014 RP

Proli Footwear
Interest Analyses
December 31, 2014

	Balance per Client	Balance per Audit	Adjustment Required
Interest Expense Calculations:			
Lease L1	123,156		
Lease L2A	33,375		
Lease L2B	Operating		
Lease L3	Operating		
Lease L4	32,890		
Lease L5	28,156		
Totals	217,577		

Interest Payable Calculations:			
Lease L1	0		
Lease L2A	0		
Lease L2B	0		
Lease L3	0		
Lease L4	0		
Lease L5	0		
Totals	0		

Proli Footwear
Lease L1 Amortization Schedule

Date	Monthly Lease Payment		Reduction of Lease Obligation		Interest		Lease Obligation Balance	
5/28/01 Inception of Lease					13% EB-8		1,042,810.16 EB-2	
12/1/13	11,378.00	EB-2	1,027.75	R	10,350.25 R		954,380.25 R	
1/1/14	11,378.00		1,038.88	R	10,339.12 R		953,341.37 R	
2/1/14	11,378.00		1,050.14	R	10,327.86 R	a)	952,291.23 R	
3/1/14	11,378.00		1,061.51	R	10,316.49 R	a)	951,229.72 R	
4/1/14	11,378.00		1,073.01	R	10,304.99 R	a)	950,156.71 R	
5/1/14	11,378.00		1,084.64	R	10,293.36 R	a)	949,072.08 R	
6/1/14	11,378.00		1,096.39	R	10,281.61 R	a)	947,975.69 R	
7/1/14	11,378.00		1,108.26	R	10,269.74 R	a)	946,867.43 R	
8/1/14	11,378.00		1,120.27	R	10,257.73 R	a)	945,747.16 R	
9/1/14	11,378.00		1,132.41	R	10,245.59 R	a)	944,614.75 R	
10/1/14	11,378.00		1,144.67	R	10,233.33 R	a)	943,470.08 R	
11/1/14	11,378.00		1,157.07	R	10,220.93 R	a)	942,313.00 R	
12/1/14	11,378.00		1,169.61	R	10,208.39 R	a)	941,143.39 R	c)
1/1/15	11,378.00		1,182.28	R	b) 10,195.72 R	a)	939,961.11 R	
2/1/15	11,378.00		1,195.09	R	b) 10,182.91 R		938,766.03 R	
3/1/15	11,378.00		1,208.03	R	b) 10,169.97 R		937,557.99 R	
4/1/15	11,378.00		1,221.12	R	b) 10,156.88 R		936,336.87 R	
5/1/15	11,378.00		1,234.35	R	b) 10,143.65 R		935,102.52 R	
6/1/15	11,378.00		1,247.72	R	b) 10,130.28 R		933,854.80 R	
7/1/15	11,378.00		1,261.24	R	b) 10,116.76 R		932,593.56 R	
8/1/15	11,378.00		1,274.90	R	b) 10,103.10 R		931,318.65 R	
9/1/15	11,378.00		1,288.71	R	b) 10,089.29 R		930,029.94 R	
10/1/15	11,378.00		1,302.68	R	b) 10,075.32 R		928,727.26 R	
11/1/15	11,378.00		1,316.79	R	b) 10,061.21 R		927,410.48 R	
12/1/15	11,378.00		1,331.05	R	b) 10,046.95 R		926,079.42 R	
1/1/16	11,378.00		1,345.47	R	10,032.53 R		924,733.95 R	
2/1/16	11,378.00		1,360.05	R	10,017.95 R		923,373.90 R	

IF CAPITAL LEASE		IF OPERATING LEASE	
2014 Interest expense =	123,156 Σa)	2014 Interest expense =	$0
2014 Current maturity =	15,064 Σb)	2014 Current maturity =	$0
2014 Long-term portion =	926,079 c) - Σb)	2014 Long-term portion =	$0
2014 Interest Payable =	10,196 d)	2014 Interest Payable =	$0

R = Verified calculation by recomputation using incremental borrowing rate shown above.
L = Examined lease agreement and agreed information to the lease.
Note: Complete lease amortization schedule is included in permanent file along with copy of lease. I have verified the calculations for all months. RP

NOTE FROM RP: I have recalculated all the amounts - all you need to do is determine the classification of the lease

Proli Footwear
Lease L2A Amortization Schedule

Date	Monthly Lease Payment		Reduction of Lease Obligation			Interest		Lease Obligation Balance	
7/28/06 Inception of Lease						10% EB-8		943,405.56 EB-3	
12/1/13	11,880.00	EB-3	8,546.22	R		3,333.78 R		391,507.37 R	
1/1/14	11,880.00		8,617.44	R		3,262.56 R		382,889.93 R	
2/1/14	11,880.00		8,689.25	R		3,190.75 R a)		374,200.68 R	
3/1/14	11,880.00		8,761.66	R		3,118.34 R a)		365,439.02 R	
4/1/14	11,880.00		8,834.67	R		3,045.33 R a)		356,604.35 R	
5/1/14	11,880.00		8,908.30	R		2,971.70 R a)		347,696.05 R	
6/1/14	11,880.00		8,982.53	R		2,897.47 R a)		338,713.51 R	
7/1/14	11,880.00		9,057.39	R		2,822.61 R a)		329,656.13 R	
8/1/14	11,880.00		9,132.87	R		2,747.13 R a)		320,523.26 R	
9/1/14	11,880.00		9,208.97	R		2,671.03 R a)		311,314.29 R	
10/1/14	11,880.00		9,285.71	R		2,594.29 R a)		302,028.57 R	
11/1/14	11,880.00		9,363.10	R		2,516.90 R a)		292,665.48 R	
12/1/14	11,880.00		9,441.12	R		2,438.88 R a)		283,224.36 R c)	
1/1/15	11,880.00		9,519.80	R b)		2,360.20 R a)		273,704.56 R	
2/1/15	11,880.00		9,599.13	R b)		2,280.87 R		264,105.43 R	
3/1/15	11,880.00		9,679.12	R b)		2,200.88 R		254,426.31 R	
4/1/15	11,880.00		9,759.78	R b)		2,120.22 R		244,666.53 R	
5/1/15	11,880.00		9,841.11	R b)		2,038.89 R		234,825.42 R	
6/1/15	11,880.00		9,923.12	R b)		1,956.88 R		224,902.30 R	
7/1/15	11,880.00		10,005.81	R b)		1,874.19 R		214,896.48 R	
8/1/15	11,880.00		10,089.20	R b)		1,790.80 R		204,807.29 R	
9/1/15	11,880.00		10,173.27	R b)		1,706.73 R		194,634.01 R	
10/1/15	11,880.00		10,258.05	R b)		1,621.95 R		184,375.96 R	
11/1/15	11,880.00		10,343.53	R b)		1,536.47 R		174,032.43 R	
12/1/15	11,880.00		10,429.73	R b)		1,450.27 R		163,602.70 R	
1/1/16	11,880.00		10,516.64	R		1,363.36 R		153,086.06 R	
2/1/16	11,880.00		10,604.28	R		1,275.72 R		142,481.77 R	

IF CAPITAL LEASE		IF OPERATING LEASE	
2014 Interest expense =	33,375 Σa)	2014 Interest expense =	$0
2014 Current maturity =	119,622 Σb)	2014 Current maturity =	$0
2014 Long-term portion =	163,602 c) - Σb)	2014 Long-term portion =	$0
2014 Interest Payable =	2,360 d)	2014 Interest Payable =	$0

R = Verified calculation by recomputation using incremental borrowing rate shown above.

L = Examined lease agreement and agreed information to the lease.

Note: Complete lease amortization schedule is included in permanent file along with copy of lease. I have verified the calculations for all months.   RP

NOTE FROM RP: I have recalculated all the amounts - all you need to do is determine the classification of the lease

Proli Footwear
Lease L2B Amortization Schedule

Date	Monthly Lease Payment	Reduction of Lease Obligation	Interest	Lease Obligation Balance
1/1/14	Inception of Lease		10% EB-8	160,570.14
1/1/14	14,000.00 EB-4	14,000.00 R	0.00 R	146,570.14R
2/1/14	14,000.00	12,778.58 R	1,221.42 R a)	133,791.56R
3/1/14	14,000.00	12,885.07 R	1,114.93 R a)	120,906.49R
4/1/14	14,000.00	12,992.45 R	1,007.55 R a)	107,914.04R
5/1/14	14,000.00	13,100.72 R	899.28 R a)	94,813.33R
6/1/14	14,000.00	13,209.89 R	790.11 R a)	81,603.44R
7/1/14	14,000.00	13,319.97 R	680.03 R a)	68,283.46R
8/1/14	14,000.00	13,430.97 R	569.03 R a)	54,852.49R
9/1/14	14,000.00	13,542.90 R	457.10 R a)	41,309.60R
10/1/14	14,000.00	13,655.75 R	344.25 R a)	27,653.84R
11/1/14	14,000.00	13,769.55 R	230.45 R a)	13,884.29R
12/1/14	14,000.00	13,884.30 R	115.70 R a)	0.00R

IF CAPITAL LEASE		IF OPERATING LEASE	
2014 Interest expense =	7,430 Σa)	2014 Interest expense =	$0
2014 Current maturity	$0	2014 Current maturity =	$0
2014 Long-term	$0	2014 Long-term portion =	$0
2014 Interest Payable =	$0	2014 Interest Payable =	$0

L = Examined lease agreement and agreed information to the lease.

Note: Complete lease amortization schedule is included in permanent file along with copy of lease. I have verified the calculations for all months.   RP

NOTE FROM RP: I have recalculated all the amounts - all you need to do is determine the classification of the lease

153

Proli Footwear
Lease L3 Amortization Schedule

Date	Monthly Lease Payment		Reduction of Lease Obligation			Interest		Lease Obligation Balance	
2/28/01 Inception of Lease						13%	EB-8	377,089.25	EB-5
12/1/13	4,540.00	EB-5	2,620.87	R		1,919.13	R	174,529.66	R
1/1/14	4,540.00		2,649.26	R		1,890.74	R	171,880.40	R
2/1/14	4,540.00		2,677.96	R		1,862.04	R a)	169,202.44	R
3/1/14	4,540.00		2,706.97	R		1,833.03	R a)	166,495.46	R
4/1/14	4,540.00		2,736.30	R		1,803.70	R a)	163,759.16	R
5/1/14	4,540.00		2,765.94	R		1,774.06	R a)	160,993.22	R
6/1/14	4,540.00		2,795.91	R		1,744.09	R a)	158,197.31	R
7/1/14	4,540.00		2,826.20	R		1,713.80	R a)	155,371.12	R
8/1/14	4,540.00		2,856.81	R		1,683.19	R a)	152,514.31	R
9/1/14	4,540.00		2,887.76	R		1,652.24	R a)	149,626.54	R
10/1/14	4,540.00		2,919.05	R		1,620.95	R a)	146,707.50	R
11/1/14	4,540.00		2,950.67	R		1,589.33	R a)	143,756.83	R
12/1/14	4,540.00		2,982.63	R		1,557.37	R a)	140,774.19	R c)
1/1/15	4,540.00		3,014.95	R b)		1,525.05	R a)	137,759.25	R
2/1/15	4,540.00		3,047.61	R b)		1,492.39	R	134,711.64	R
3/1/15	4,540.00		3,080.62	R b)		1,459.38	R	131,631.02	R
4/1/15	4,540.00		3,114.00	R b)		1,426.00	R	128,517.02	R
5/1/15	4,540.00		3,147.73	R b)		1,392.27	R	125,369.29	R
6/1/15	4,540.00		3,181.83	R b)		1,358.17	R	122,187.45	R
7/1/15	4,540.00		3,216.30	R b)		1,323.70	R	118,971.15	R
8/1/15	4,540.00		3,251.15	R b)		1,288.85	R	115,720.01	R
9/1/15	4,540.00		3,286.37	R b)		1,253.63	R	112,433.64	R
10/1/15	4,540.00		3,321.97	R b)		1,218.03	R	109,111.67	R
11/1/15	4,540.00		3,357.96	R b)		1,182.04	R	105,753.71	R
12/1/15	4,540.00		3,394.33	R b)		1,145.67	R	102,359.38	R
1/1/16	103,468.27		102,359.38	R		1,108.89	R	0.00	R

IF CAPITAL LEASE		IF OPERATING LEASE	
2014 Interest expense =	20,359 Σa)	2014 Interest expense =	$0
2014 Current maturity	38,415 Σb)	2014 Current maturity =	$0
2014 Long-term	102,359 c) - Σb)	2014 Long-term portion =	$0
2014 Interest Payable =	1,525 d)	2014 Interest Payable =	$0

R = Verified calculation by recomputation using incremental borrowing rate shown above.

L = Examined lease agreement and agreed information to the lease.

Note: Complete lease amortization schedule is included in permanent file along with copy of lease.

I have verified the calculations for all months.   RP

NOTE FROM RP: I have recalculated all the amounts - all you need to do is determine the classification of the lease

Proli Footwear
Lease L4 Amortization Schedule

Date	Monthly Lease Payment		Reduction of Lease Obligation		Interest		Lease Obligation Balance	
8/28/12 Inception of Lease					13%	EB-8	1.064.826.03	EB-6
12/1/13	13,330.00	EB-6	9,760.33	R	3,569.67	R	319,747.30	R
1/1/14	13,330.00		9,866.07	R	3,463.93	R	309,881.23	R
2/1/14	13,330.00		9,972.95	R	3,357.05	R a)	299,908.28	R
3/1/14	13,330.00		10,080.99	R	3,249.01	R a)	289,827.28	R
4/1/14	13,330.00		10,190.20	R	3,139.80	R a)	279,637.08	R
5/1/14	13,330.00		10,300.60	R	3,029.40	R a)	269,336.48	R
6/1/14	13,330.00		10,412.19	R	2,917.81	R a)	258,924.29	R
7/1/14	13,330.00		10,524.99	R	2,805.01	R a)	248,399.30	R
8/1/14	13,330.00		10,639.01	R	2,690.99	R a)	237,760.30	R
9/1/14	13,330.00		10,754.26	R	2,575.74	R a)	227,006.03	R
10/1/14	13,330.00		10,870.77	R	2,459.23	R a)	216,135.27	R
11/1/14	13,330.00		10,988.53	R	2,341.47	R a)	205,146.73	R
12/1/14	13,330.00		11,107.58	R	2,222.42	R a)	194,039.15	R c)
1/1/15	13,330.00		11,227.91	R b)	2,102.09	R a)	182,811.24	R
2/1/15	13,330.00		11,349.54	R b)	1,980.46	R	171,461.70	R
3/1/15	13,330.00		11,472.50	R b)	1,857.50	R	159,989.20	R
4/1/15	13,330.00		11,596.78	R b)	1,733.22	R	148,392.42	R
4/1/15	150,000.00		148,392.42	R b)	1,607.58	R	0.00	R

IF CAPITAL LEASE			IF OPERATING LEASE	
2014 Interest expense =	32,890 Σa)		2014 Interest expense =	$0
2014 Current maturity	194,039 Σb)		2014 Current maturity =	$0
2014 Long-term	$0 c)- Σb)		2014 Long-term portion =	$0
2014 Interest Payable =	2,102 d)		2014 Interest Payable =	$0

R = Verified calculation by recomputation using incremental borrowing rate shown above.

L = Examined lease agreement and agreed information to the lease.

Note: Complete lease amortization schedule is included in permanent file along with copy of lease.
I have verified the calculations for all months.   RP

NOTE FROM RP: I have recalculated all the amounts - all you need to do is determine the classification of the lease

Proli Footwear
Lease L5 Amortization Schedule

Date	Monthly Lease Payment		Reduction of Lease Obligation		Interest		Lease Obligation Balance
7/28/06 Inception of Lease					9% EB-8		438,946.34 EB-7
12/1/13	8,057.00	EB-7	5,397.63	R	2,659.37	R	349,185.50 R
1/1/14	8,057.00		5,438.11	R	2,618.89	R	343,747.39 R
2/1/14	8,057.00		5,478.89	R	2,578.11	R a)	338,268.50 R
3/1/14	8,057.00		5,519.99	R	2,537.01	R a)	332,748.51 R
4/1/14	8,057.00		5,561.39	R	2,495.61	R a)	327,187.12 R
5/1/14	8,057.00		5,603.10	R	2,453.90	R a)	321,584.03 R
6/1/14	8,057.00		5,645.12	R	2,411.88	R a)	315,938.91 R
7/1/14	8,057.00		5,687.46	R	2,369.54	R a)	310,251.45 R
8/1/14	8,057.00		5,730.11	R	2,326.89	R a)	304,521.34 R
9/1/14	8,057.00		5,773.09	R	2,283.91	R a)	298,748.25 R
10/1/14	8,057.00		5,816.39	R	2,240.61	R a)	292,931.86 R
11/1/14	8,057.00		5,860.01	R	2,196.99	R a)	287,071.85 R
12/1/14	8,057.00		5,903.96	R	2,153.04	R a)	281,167.89 R c)
1/1/15	8,057.00		5,948.24	R b)	2,108.76	R a)	275,219.64 R
2/1/15	8,057.00		5,992.85	R b)	2,064.15	R	269,226.79 R
3/1/15	8,057.00		6,037.80	R b)	2,019.20	R	263,188.99 R
4/1/15	8,057.00		6,083.08	R b)	1,973.92	R	257,105.91 R
5/1/15	8,057.00		6,128.71	R b)	1,928.29	R	250,977.20 R
6/1/15	8,057.00		6,174.67	R b)	1,882.33	R	244,802.53 R
7/1/15	8,057.00		6,220.98	R b)	1,836.02	R	238,581.55 R
8/1/15	8,057.00		6,267.64	R b)	1,789.36	R	232,313.91 R
9/1/15	8,057.00		6,314.65	R b)	1,742.35	R	225,999.27 R
10/1/15	8,057.00		6,362.01	R b)	1,694.99	R	219,637.26 R
11/1/15	8,057.00		6,409.72	R b)	1,647.28	R	213,227.54 R
12/1/15	8,057.00		6,457.79	R b)	1,599.21	R	206,769.75 R
1/1/16	8,057.00		6,506.23	R	1,550.77	R	200,263.52 R
2/1/16	8,057.00		6,555.02	R	1,501.98	R	193,708.50 R

IF CAPITAL LEASE		IF OPERATING LEASE	
2014 Interest expense =	28,156 Σa)	2014 Interest expense =	$0
2014 Current maturity =	74,398 Σb)	2014 Current maturity =	$0
2014 Long-term portion =	206,770 c)- Σb)	2014 Long-term portion =	$0
2014 Interest Payable =	2,109 d)	2014 Interest Payable =	$0

R = verified calculation by recomputation using incremental borrowing rate shown above.

L = Examined lease agreement and agreed information to the lease.

Note: Complete lease amortization schedule is included in permanent file along with copy of lease. I have verified the calculations for all months. RP

NOTE FROM RP: I have recalculated all the amounts - all you need to do is determine the classification of the lease

Proli Footwear
AJE Control-Lease Liabilities
December 31, 2014

AJE Number	Reference	Accounts/Description	Account Number	Debit	Credit

x = account has impact on income before taxes amount
Impact on income before taxes =   DR/CR

Proli Footwear
Red Flag Events-Lease Liabilities
December 31, 2014

Event Number	Reference	Auditor Observation

Proli Footwear
Management Letter Comments-Lease Liabilities
December 31, 2014

Comment Number	Reference	Auditor Observation/ Recommendation	Benefit to Client

Proli Footwear
Time Control
December 31, 2014

Section	Budgeted Time	Time Spent Working with Team	Time Spent Working Alone
7B. Lease Liabilities	3 hours		

Team member names:

ASSIGNMENT #7C – MORTGAGE LIABILITIES

ASSIGNMENT

1. Complete each step of the mortgage liabilities audit program. Indicate completion by initialing and dating each step that has not been completed. For those audit program steps that are already initialed as having been completed, enter an appropriate date next to the initials.

2. Be sure to use the appropriate tickmarks to indicate the specific work performed on each piece of audit documentation.

3. Complete and submit for grading all the audit documentation for this section organized in the following sequence:
   a. Audit program with dates, initials and audit documentation references;
   b. Completed Lead Schedule with workpaper references, tickmarks indicating work done and appropriate sign-offs;
   c. Specific audit workpaper schedules in sequence with workpaper references, as appropriate, tickmarks indicating work done and appropriate sign-offs;
   d. Adjusting Journal Entry Control containing the proposed AJEs;
   e. Red Flag Events;
   f. Management Letter Comments containing recommended improvements to internal control and other operating issues;
   g. Updated Time Control Worksheet; and
   h. Updated Working Trial Balance (WTB).

4. Each adjusting entry should be entered on the following audit documentation:
   a. Appropriate workpaper schedule
   b. Lead schedule
   c. AJE control
   d. Working trial balance

AUDIT PROGRAM – MORTGAGE LIABILITIES

Procedures	Initials	Date	W/P Ref
General			
1. Foot and crossfoot lead schedule and all other PBC schedules.			
2. Compare balances on other PBC schedules with balances on the lead schedules.			
3. Compare balances on lead schedule with account balances in the trial balance.			

Procedures	Initials	Date	W/P Ref

Analytical Review Procedures

1. Review entries to liability and related accounts for the period and investigate large or unusual items. — RP

2. Review minutes for authorization for borrowings — RP — 2/15 — EC-3

Substantive Audit Procedures

1. Confirm debt. — RP

Mortgages Payable

2. Recalculate current portion of mortgages payable.

3. Review clerical accuracy of carrying value of long-term debt.

4. Compare amount confirmed by bank with audit documentation and lead schedule.

5. Review for proper financial statement classification and disclosure.

6. Recalculate interest expense.

HELPFUL HINTS FROM THE IN-CHARGE ACCOUNTANT:

1. Use a tickmark to show each work procedure performed.

2. Remember to post adjusting entries affecting mortgage liabilities from previous sections to the mortgage liabilities lead sheet.

3. Be alert for "Red Flag" events. A red flag event is an event or transaction that might indicate fraudulent activity, but needs further investigation to determine:
   a. Whether it was intentional or just human error and
   b. The impact of the event.

4. All debt amortization schedules are based on the annuity due concept of amortization. All debt amortization schedules are based on the annuity due concept of amortization. Please refer to an accounting text to refresh your understanding of annuity due versus annuity in advance.

5. Remember that any work RP has completed need not be repeated by you. You may assume that RP has done all the necessary work to complete the work program step correctly. *All of RP's work looks like this.*

Proli Footwear
Lead Schedule - Mortgage Liabilities
December 31, 2014

Account Number	Account Title	Balance per T/B Debit	Balance per T/B Credit	Adjustments Debit	Adjustments Credit	Balance per Audit Debit	Balance per Audit Credit
Current Maturities of Mortgages							
	Mortgage 1		6,710				
	Mortgage 2		14,017				
	Mortgage 3		4,486				
	Mortgage 4		12,782				
2120	Total Current Maturities		37,995				
Mortgages Payable							
	Mortgage 1		1,729,200				
	Mortgage 2		869,441				
	Mortgage 3		637,216				
	Mortgage 4		1,430,146				
2520	Total Mortgages		4,666,003				
Related Accounts							
2412	Interest Payable-Mortgages		0				
8310	Interest Expense	485,472					

Impact of AJEs for this assignment on net income before income taxes = _____ DR/CR

163

©Proctor and Poli

Proli Footwear
Mortgages Payable
December 31, 2014

Description	Balance per Client	Balance per Bank	Audit Adjustment
Current Maturities of Mortgages			
Mortgage 1	6,710		
Mortgage 2	14,017		
Mortgage 3	4,486		
Mortgage 4	12,782		
Long-Term Portion of Mortgages			
Mortgage 1	1,729,200		
Mortgage 2	869,441		
Mortgage 3	637,216		
Mortgage 4	1,430,146		

Proli Footwear
Debt Information
December 31, 2014

Collateral	Date of Loan	Amount Borrowed	Interest Rate	Term	Monthly Payment	Bank
Mortgage 1 ᴹ Land and buildings - Proli, CT	04/01/96 ∨	2,275,650∨	12%	360 months ∨	23,408	Local National Bank
Mortgage 2 ᴹ Land and buildings - Walton, FL	10/01/01 ∨	962,300∨	14%	360 months ∨	11,402	Walton Trust
Mortgage 3 ᴹ Land and buildings - Walton, FL	02/01/11 ∨	654,990∨	11%	360 months ∨	6,238	Walton Trust
Mortgage 4 ᴹ Land and building - Proli, CT	04/01/14 ∨	1,450,900∨	8%	360 months ∨	10,646	Local National Bank

ᴹ = Traced authorization to the Board of Directors' minutes.

∨ = Verified information by examining the mortgage contract

165

Proli Footwear
Interest Analyses
December 31, 2014

	Balance per Client	Balance per Audit	Adjustment Required
Interest Expense Calculations:			
Mortgage 1	212,815		
Mortgage 2	124,629		
Mortgage 3	70,831		
Mortgage 4	77,197		
Totals	485,472		
Interest Payable Calculations:			
Mortgage 1	0		
Mortgage 2	0		
Mortgage 3	0		
Mortgage 4	0		
Totals	0		

PROLI FOOTWEAR
STAMFORD, CONNECTICUT

January 5, 2015

Local National Bank
Proli, CT

Dear Sirs:

Our independent auditors, West & Fair CPAs, LLC, are performing an audit of our financial statements. We have provided our accountants with information regarding deposit and loan balances as of *December 31, 2014*. Please confirm the accuracy of this information, noting any discrepancies in the information provided. If other balances are outstanding, please include that information. Please return this letter directly to our accountants: *West & Fair CPAs, LLC; Stamford, CT*

1. Deposit information

Account Name	Account No.	Interest Rate	Balance
None			

2. Loan information

Account No. Description	Balance	Monthly Payment	Date Due	Interest Rate	Date through Which Interest Is Paid	Description of Collateral
Mortgage #1	$1,735,910	$23,407.62	Monthly	12%	12/1/2014	Land & Buildings – Proli, CT
Mortgage #4	$1,442,928	$10,646.19	Monthly	8%	12/1/2014	

Very truly yours,
Harold F. Heele
Harold F. Heele
Vice President – Finance and Chief Financial Officer

CONFIRMATION: The information presented above is in agreement with our records. Although we have not performed a detailed search of our records, no other deposit or loan accounts have come to our attention except as noted below.

Exceptions or Comments:
...None...
....

John Smith	*January 11, 2013*	*Bank Manager*
(Institution's Authorized Signature)	(Date)	(Title)

Local National Bank
Attachment to Bank Confirmation
Mortgage Loan Amortization Schedule

Mortgage 1

Payment #	Date	Monthly Payment	Principal Reduction	Interest	Mortgage Payable Balance
212	12/01/13	23,407.62	5,314.60 ℞	18,093.02 ℞	1,803,986.96 ℞
213	01/01/14	23,407.62	5,367.75 ℞	18,039.87 ℞	1,798,619.21 ℞
214	02/01/14	23,407.62	5,421.43 ℞	17,986.19 ℞ a)	1,793,197.78 ℞
215	03/01/14	23,407.62	5,475.64 ℞	17,931.98 ℞ a)	1,787,722.14 ℞
216	04/01/14	23,407.62	5,530.40 ℞	17,877.22 ℞ a)	1,782,191.74 ℞
217	05/01/14	23,407.62	5,585.70 ℞	17,821.92 ℞ a)	1,776,606.04 ℞
218	06/01/14	23,407.62	5,641.56 ℞	17,766.06 ℞ a)	1,770,964.48 ℞
219	07/01/14	23,407.62	5,697.98 ℞	17,709.64 ℞ a)	1,765,266.50 ℞
220	08/01/14	23,407.62	5,754.95 ℞	17,652.67 ℞ a)	1,759,511.55 ℞
221	09/01/14	23,407.62	5,812.50 ℞	17,595.12 ℞ a)	1,753,699.04 ℞
222	10/01/14	23,407.62	5,870.63 ℞	17,536.99 ℞ a)	1,747,828.41 ℞
223	11/01/14	23,407.62	5,929.34 ℞	17,478.28 ℞ a)	1,741,899.08 ℞
224	12/01/14	23,407.62	5,988.63 ℞	17,418.99 ℞ a)	1,735,910.45 ℞
225	01/01/15	23,407.62	6,048.52 ℞ b)	17,359.10 ℞ a) d)	1,729,861.93 ℞ c)
226	02/01/15	23,407.62	6,109.00 ℞ b)	17,298.62 ℞	1,723,752.93 ℞
227	03/01/15	23,407.62	6,170.09 ℞ b)	17,237.53 ℞	1,717,582.84 ℞
228	04/01/15	23,407.62	6,231.79 ℞ b)	17,175.83 ℞	1,711,351.05 ℞
229	05/01/15	23,407.62	6,294.11 ℞ b)	17,113.51 ℞	1,705,056.94 ℞
230	06/01/15	23,407.62	6,357.05 ℞ b)	17,050.57 ℞	1,698,699.89 ℞
231	07/01/15	23,407.62	6,420.62 ℞ b)	16,987.00 ℞	1,692,279.27 ℞
232	08/01/15	23,407.62	6,484.83 ℞ b)	16,922.79 ℞	1,685,794.44 ℞
233	09/01/15	23,407.62	6,549.68 ℞ b)	16,857.94 ℞	1,679,244.77 ℞
234	10/01/15	23,407.62	6,615.17 ℞ b)	16,792.45 ℞	1,672,629.59 ℞
235	11/01/15	23,407.62	6,681.32 ℞ b)	16,726.30 ℞	1,665,948.27 ℞
236	12/01/15	23,407.62	6,748.14 ℞ b)	16,659.48 ℞	1,659,200.13 ℞
237	01/01/16	23,407.62	6,815.62 ℞	16,592.00 ℞	1,652,384.51 ℞
238	02/01/16	23,407.62	6,883.77 ℞	16,523.85 ℞	1,645,500.74 ℞

John Smith
_____
(Institution's Authorized Signature)

January 11, 2015
_____
(Date)

Bank Manager
_____
(Title)

2014 Interest expense =	212,134	Σa)
2014 Current maturity =	76,710	Σb)
2014 Long-term portion =	1,659,200	c)-Σb)
2014 Interest payable =	17,359	d)

℞ = Verified calculation by recomputation using interest rate of 12%.

Local National Bank
Attachment to Bank Confirmation
Mortgage Loan Amortization Schedule

Mortgage 4

Payment #	Date	Monthly Payment	Principal Reduction		Interest		Mortgage Payable Balance	
1	05/01/14	10,646.19	973.52	ℛ	9,672.67	ℛ a)	1,449,926.48	ℛ
2	06/01/14	10,646.19	980.01	ℛ	9,666.18	ℛ a)	1,448,946.47	ℛ
3	07/01/14	10,646.19	986.55	ℛ	9,659.64	ℛ a)	1,447,959.92	ℛ
4	08/01/14	10,646.19	993.12	ℛ	9,653.07	ℛ a)	1,446,966.80	ℛ
5	09/01/14	10,646.19	999.74	ℛ	9,646.45	ℛ a)	1,445,967.05	ℛ
6	10/01/14	10,646.19	1,006.41	ℛ	9,639.78	ℛ a)	1,444,960.64	ℛ
7	11/01/14	10,646.19	1,013.12	ℛ	9,633.07	ℛ a)	1,443,947.52	ℛ
8	12/01/14	10,646.19	1,019.87	ℛ	9,626.32	ℛ a)	1,442,927.65	ℛ
9	01/01/15	10,646.19	1,026.67	ℛ b)	9,619.52	ℛ a) d)	1,441,900.98	ℛ c)
10	02/01/15	10,646.19	1,033.52	ℛ b)	9,612.67	ℛ	1,440,867.46	ℛ
11	03/01/15	10,646.19	1,040.41	ℛ b)	9,605.78	ℛ	1,439,827.05	ℛ
12	04/01/15	10,646.19	1,047.34	ℛ b)	9,598.85	ℛ	1,438,779.71	ℛ
13	05/01/15	10,646.19	1,054.33	ℛ b)	9,591.86	ℛ	1,437,725.38	ℛ
14	06/01/15	10,646.19	1,061.35	ℛ b)	9,584.84	ℛ	1,436,664.03	ℛ
15	07/01/15	10,646.19	1,068.43	ℛ b)	9,577.76	ℛ	1,435,595.60	ℛ
16	08/01/15	10,646.19	1,075.55	ℛ b)	9,570.64	ℛ	1,434,520.05	ℛ
17	09/01/15	10,646.19	1,082.72	ℛ b)	9,563.47	ℛ	1,433,437.33	ℛ
18	10/01/15	10,646.19	1,089.94	ℛ b)	9,556.25	ℛ	1,432,347.38	ℛ
19	11/01/15	10,646.19	1,097.21	ℛ b)	9,548.98	ℛ	1,431,250.18	ℛ
20	12/01/15	10,646.19	1,104.52	ℛ b)	9,541.67	ℛ	1,430,145.65	ℛ
21	01/01/16	10,646.19	1,111.89	ℛ	9,534.30	ℛ	1,429,033.77	ℛ
22	02/01/16	10,646.19	1,119.30	ℛ	9,526.89	ℛ	1,427,914.47	ℛ

John Smith
(Institution's Authorized Signature)

January 11, 2015
(Date)

Bank Manager
(Title)

2014 Interest expense =	86,817	Σa)
2014 Current maturity =	12,782	Σb)
2014 Long-term portion =	1,430,146	c)-Σb)
2014 Interest payable =	9,620	d)

ℛ = verified calculation by recomputation using interest rate of 8%.

PROLI FOOTWEAR
STAMFORD, CONNECTICUT

January 5, 2015

Walton Trust
Walton, FL

Dear Sirs:

Our independent auditors, West & Fair CPAs, LLC, are performing an audit of our financial statements. We have provided our accountants with information regarding deposit and loan balances as of *December 31, 2014*. Please confirm the accuracy of this information, noting any discrepancies in the information provided. If other balances are outstanding, please include that information. Please return this letter directly to our accountants: *West & Fair CPAs, LLC; Stamford, CT*

3. Deposit information

Account Name	Account No.	Interest Rate	Balance
None			

4. Loan information

Account No. Description	Balance	Monthly Payment	Date Due	Interest Rate	Date through Which Interest Is Paid	Description of Collateral
Mortgage #2	$ 883,458	$11,402.02	Monthly	14%	12/1/2014	Land & Buildings - Walton, FL
Mortgage #3	$ 641,702	$ 6,237.62	Monthly	11%	12/1/2014	
Note Payable	$12,800,000	N/A	3/1/2016	11%	12/31/2014	None

Very truly yours,
Harold F. Heele
Harold F. Heele
Vice President – Finance and Chief Financial Officer

CONFIRMATION: The information presented above is in agreement with our records. Although we have not performed a detailed search of our records, no other deposit or loan accounts have come to our attention except as noted below.

Exceptions or Comments:
…None……………………………………………………………………………………………………

Mary Jones	*January 14, 2015*	*Bank Manager*
(Institution's Authorized Signature)	(Date)	(Title)

Walton Trust
Attachment to Bank Confirmation
Mortgage Loan Amortization Schedule

Mortgage 2

Payment #	Date	Monthly Payment	Principal Reduction	Interest	Mortgage Payable Balance	
146	12/01/13	11,402.02	941.74 ℞	10,460.28 ℞	895,653.92	℞
147	01/01/14	11,402.02	952.72 ℞	10,449.30 ℞	894,701.20	℞
148	02/01/14	11,402.02	963.84 ℞	10,438.18 ℞ a)	893,737.36	℞
149	03/01/14	11,402.02	975.08 ℞	10,426.94 ℞ a)	892,762.27	℞
150	04/01/14	11,402.02	986.46 ℞	10,415.56 ℞ a)	891,775.81	℞
151	05/01/14	11,402.02	997.97 ℞	10,404.05 ℞ a)	890,777.84	℞
152	06/01/14	11,402.02	1,009.61 ℞	10,392.41 ℞ a)	889,768.23	℞
153	07/01/14	11,402.02	1,021.39 ℞	10,380.63 ℞ a)	888,746.84	℞
154	08/01/14	11,402.02	1,033.31 ℞	10,368.71 ℞ a)	887,713.53	℞
155	09/01/14	11,402.02	1,045.36 ℞	10,356.66 ℞ a)	886,668.17	℞
156	10/01/14	11,402.02	1,057.56 ℞	10,344.46 ℞ a)	885,610.61	℞
157	11/01/14	11,402.02	1,069.90 ℞	10,332.12 ℞ a)	884,540.72	℞
158	12/01/14	11,402.02	1,082.38 ℞	10,319.64 ℞ a)	883,458.34	℞
159	01/01/15	11,402.02	1,095.01 ℞ b)	10,307.01 ℞ a) d)	882,363.33	℞ c)
160	02/01/15	11,402.02	1,107.78 ℞ b)	10,294.24 ℞	881,255.55	℞
161	03/01/15	11,402.02	1,120.71 ℞ b)	10,281.31 ℞	880,134.85	℞
162	04/01/15	11,402.02	1,133.78 ℞ b)	10,268.24 ℞	879,001.07	℞
163	05/01/15	11,402.02	1,147.01 ℞ b)	10,255.01 ℞	877,854.06	℞
164	06/01/15	11,402.02	1,160.39 ℞ b)	10,241.63 ℞	876,693.67	℞
165	07/01/15	11,402.02	1,173.93 ℞ b)	10,228.09 ℞	875,519.74	℞
166	08/01/15	11,402.02	1,187.62 ℞ b)	10,214.40 ℞	874,332.12	℞
167	09/01/15	11,402.02	1,201.48 ℞ b)	10,200.54 ℞	873,130.64	℞
168	10/01/15	11,402.02	1,215.50 ℞ b)	10,186.52 ℞	871,915.15	℞
169	11/01/15	11,402.02	1,229.68 ℞ b)	10,172.34 ℞	870,685.47	℞
170	12/01/15	11,402.02	1,244.02 ℞ b)	10,158.00 ℞	869,441.45	℞
171	01/01/16	11,402.02	1,258.54 ℞	10,143.48 ℞	868,182.91	℞
172	02/01/16	11,402.02	1,273.22 ℞	10,128.80 ℞	866,909.69	℞

Mary Janes   *January 14, 2015*   *Bank Manager*

(Institution's Authorized Signature)   (Date)   (Title)

2014 Interest expense =   124,486   Σa)

2014 Current maturity =   14,017   Σb)

2014 Long-term portion=   869,441   c)-Σb)

2014 Interest payable =   10,307   d)

℞ = verified calculation by recomputation using interest rate of 14%.

Walton Trust
Attachment to Bank Confirmation
Mortgage Loan Amortization Schedule

Mortgage 3

Payment #	Date	Monthly Payment	Principal Reduction		Interest		Mortgage Payable Balance	
34	12/01/13	6,237.62	315.61	ℝ	5,922.01	ℝ	645,722.22	ℝ
35	01/01/14	6,237.62	318.50	ℝ	5,919.12	ℝ	645,403.72	ℝ
36	02/01/14	6,237.62	321.42	ℝ	5,916.20	ℝ a)	645,082.30	ℝ
37	03/01/14	6,237.62	324.37	ℝ	5,913.25	ℝ a)	644,757.94	ℝ
38	04/01/14	6,237.62	327.34	ℝ	5,910.28	ℝ a)	644,430.60	ℝ
39	05/01/14	6,237.62	330.34	ℝ	5,907.28	ℝ a)	644,100.26	ℝ
40	06/01/14	6,237.62	333.37	ℝ	5,904.25	ℝ a)	643,766.89	ℝ
41	07/01/14	6,237.62	336.42	ℝ	5,901.20	ℝ a)	643,430.47	ℝ
42	08/01/14	6,237.62	339.51	ℝ	5,898.11	ℝ a)	643,090.96	ℝ
43	09/01/14	6,237.62	342.62	ℝ	5,895.00	ℝ a)	642,748.34	ℝ
44	10/01/14	6,237.62	345.76	ℝ	5,891.86	ℝ a)	642,402.58	ℝ
45	11/01/14	6,237.62	348.93	ℝ	5,888.69	ℝ a)	642,053.65	ℝ
46	12/01/14	6,237.62	352.13	ℝ	5,885.49	ℝ a)	641,701.52	ℝ
47	01/01/15	6,237.62	355.36	ℝ b)	5,882.26	ℝ a) d)	641,346.16	ℝ c)
48	02/01/15	6,237.62	358.61	ℝ b)	5,879.01	ℝ	640,987.55	ℝ
49	03/01/15	6,237.62	361.90	ℝ b)	5,875.72	ℝ	640,625.65	ℝ
50	04/01/15	6,237.62	365.22	ℝ b)	5,872.40	ℝ	640,260.43	ℝ
51	05/01/15	6,237.62	368.57	ℝ b)	5,869.05	ℝ	639,891.87	ℝ
52	06/01/15	6,237.62	371.94	ℝ b)	5,865.68	ℝ	639,519.92	ℝ
53	07/01/15	6,237.62	375.35	ℝ b)	5,862.27	ℝ	639,144.57	ℝ
54	08/01/15	6,237.62	378.79	ℝ b)	5,858.83	ℝ	638,765.77	ℝ
55	09/01/15	6,237.62	382.27	ℝ b)	5,855.35	ℝ	638,383.51	ℝ
56	10/01/15	6,237.62	385.77	ℝ b)	5,851.85	ℝ	637,997.73	ℝ
57	11/01/15	6,237.62	389.31	ℝ b)	5,848.31	ℝ	637,608.43	ℝ
58	12/01/15	6,237.62	392.88	ℝ b)	5,844.74	ℝ	637,215.55	ℝ
59	01/01/16	6,237.62	396.48	ℝ	5,841.14	ℝ	636,819.07	ℝ
60	02/01/16	6,237.62	400.11	ℝ	5,837.51	ℝ	636,418.96	ℝ

Mary Janes   _January 14, 2015_   _Bank Manager_

(Institution's Authorized Signature)   (Date)   (Title)

2014 Interest expense =   70,794   Σa)
2014 Current maturity =   4,486   Σb)
2014 Long-term portion=   637,216   c)-Σb)
2014 Interest payable =   5,882   d)

ℝ = Verified calculation by recomputation using interest rate of 11%.

Proli Footwear
AJE Control-Mortgage Liabilities
December 31, 2014

AJE Number	Reference	Accounts/Description	Account Number	Debit	Credit

x = account has impact on income before taxes amount
Impact on income before taxes =   DR/CR

Proli Footwear
Red Flag Events-Mortgage Liabilities
December 31, 2014

Event Number	Reference	Auditor Observation

Proli Footwear
Management Letter Comments-Mortgage Liabilities
December 31, 2014

Comment Number	Reference	Auditor Observation/ Recommendation	Benefit to Client

Proli Footwear
Time Control
December 31, 2014

Section	Budgeted Time	Time Spent Working with Team	Time Spent Working Alone
7C. Mortgage Liabilities	3 hours		

Team member names:

ASSIGNMENT #8 – FINISHING THE AUDIT

ASSIGNMENT

1. Complete each step of the finishing the audit audit program. Indicate completion for each step by making sure that the step is initialed, dated, and that the workpaper reference is indicated. For those audit program steps that are already initialed as having been completed, enter an appropriate date and workpaper reference next to the initials.

2. Be sure to use the appropriate tickmarks to indicate the specific work performed on each piece of audit documentation.

3. Complete and submit for grading all the audit documentation for this section organized in the following sequence:
   a. Audit program with dates, initials and audit documentation references;
   b. Completed Lead Schedule with workpaper references, tickmarks indicating work done and appropriate sign-offs;
   c. Specific audit workpaper schedules in sequence with workpaper references, as appropriate, tickmarks indicating work done and appropriate sign-offs;
   d. Adjusting Journal Entry Control containing the proposed AJEs;
   e. Red Flag Events;
   f. Management Letter Comments containing recommended improvements to internal control and other operating issues;
   g. Updated Time Control Worksheet; and
   h. Updated Working Trial Balance (WTB).

4. Each adjusting entry should be entered on the following audit documentation:
   a. Appropriate workpaper schedule
   b. Lead schedule
   c. AJE control
   d. Working trial balance

AUDIT PROGRAM – FINISHING THE AUDIT

Procedures	Initials	Date	W/P Ref
General			
1. Foot and crossfoot lead schedule and all other PBC schedules.			
2. Compare balances on other PBC schedules with balances on the lead schedule.			
3. Compare balances on lead schedule with account balances in the trial balance			
Substantive Audit Procedures – Stockholders' Equity			
1. Compare list of stockholders with stock certificate book noting dates issued, certificate numbers, number of shares, and in whose name the certificates were issued .	RP	2/15	F-2
2. Review minutes for authorization for dividend declarations	RP	2/15	F-3

Procedures	Initials	Date	W/P Ref

Substantive Audit Procedures – Dividends Payable

3. Recompute amount of dividends payable.

4. Prepare adjusting journal entry, if necessary.

Substantive Audit Procedures - Income Taxes Payable

1. Examine quarterly estimated tax returns, entries in the check register, canceled checks, and postings to the account.   RP

2. Trace postings from the general journal to the account.   RP

3. Complete calculation of total income tax expense for the year, income tax payable, and deferred income taxes.

4. Prepare adjusting journal entry, if necessary.

Completing the Audit

1. Obtain the management representation letter   RP

2. Obtain and evaluate attorney representation letter.   RP

3. Review for subsequent events by extending audit procedures sufficiently to permit an opinion.   RP

   a. Make inquiries of management concerning any significant events subsequent to year-end with a potential financial   RP

   b. Examine the Board of Directors' minutes subsequent to year-end for undisclosed events with a potential financial statement impact   RP

   c. Examine legal invoices subsequent to year-end for unusual and undisclosed legal activities   RP

HELPFUL HINTS FROM THE IN-CHARGE ACCOUNTANT:

1. Use a tickmark to show each work procedure performed.
2. Remember to post adjusting entries affecting lease liabilities from previous sections to the lease liabilities lead sheet.
3. Be alert for "Red Flag" events. A red flag event is an event or transaction that might indicate fraudulent activity, but needs further investigation to determine:
   a. Whether it was intentional or just human error and
   b. The impact of the event.
3. Refer to an accounting text and review the rules relating to contingencies, subsequent events and income taxes.
4. Remember that any work RP has completed need not be repeated by you. You may assume that RP has done <u>all</u> the necessary work to complete the work program step correctly. *All of RP's work looks like this.*

Proli Footwear
Lead Schedule - Equity and Other Accounts
December 31, 2014

Account Number	Account Title	Balance per T/B Debit	Balance per T/B Credit	Adjustments Debit	Adjustments Credit	Balance per Audit Debit	Balance per Audit Credit
3000	Common Stock		50,000				
3100	Additional Paid in Capital		22,500,000				
3200	Retained Earnings		49,966,113				
3220	Prior Period Adjustment		0				
3250	Dividends Declared	1,500,000					
2420	Dividends Payable		0				
1650	Deferred Tax Asset	0					
2430	Income Tax Payable		150,000				
2700	Deferred Tax Liability		0				
8550	Settlement Loss	0					
8600	Income Tax Expense						

Impact of AJEs for this assignment on net income before income taxes = _____ DR/CR

179

Proli Footwear
List of Stockholders
December 31, 2014

Stockholder Name		Certificate Number	Date Issued	Number of Shares
Samuel Sole, Jr.	E	PS-100	4/26/1992	10,000
Samantha Sole	E	PS-101	4/26/1992	10,000
V. Jay Sole	E	PS-102	4/26/1992	10,000
Vanda Sole	E	PS-103	4/26/1992	10,000
Maureen T. Curry	E	PS-104	4/26/1992	10,000

Note: 50,000 shares of common stock were outstanding during the year. RP

E = Examined stock certificate book

Note: All stockholders are siblings. RP

Proli Footwear
Dividends Declared and Payable
December 31, 2014

	Balance per Client	Balance per Audit	Adjustment Required
Dividends Declared Calculation:			
Dividends Declared	1,500,000		
Dividends Payable Calculation:			
Dividends Payable	0		

Date Dividend Declared		Date Payable	Dividend per Share		Amount of Dividend
March 13, 2014	M	April 28, 2014	10.00	T	500,000
June 13, 2014	M	July 28, 2014	10.00	T	500,000
September 13, 2014	M	October 28, 2014	10.00	T	500,000
December 13, 2014	M	January 14, 2015	10.00		

M= Examined Board of Directors' minutes for approval and amount per share.

E = Examined stock certificate book

T = Traced payment to check register.

Note: 50,000 shares of common stock were outstanding during the year. RP

Proli Footwear
Income Tax Expense Payable Analysis
December 31, 2014

	Balance per Client	Balance per Audit	Adjustment Required
Income Tax Expense Calculation:			
4/15/14 paid 1st quarter 2014 estimate T 400,000			
6/15/14 paid 1st quarter 2014 estimate T 400,000			
9/15/14 paid 1st quarter 2014 estimate T 400,000			
12/13/1 paid 4th quarter 2014 estimate T 400,000			
Total	1,600,000		
Income Tax Payable Calculation:			
Balance - December 31, 2013 150,000			
3/11/2014 paid balance from 2013 T (150,000)			
Total	0	a)	
Income Tax Payable Calculation:			
Pretax income per financial statements:			
Permanent differences:			
Minus: Nontaxable revenue			
Plus: Nondeductible expenses			
Reversing temporary differences - Warranty work completed			
Temporary differences:			
Taxable income (loss)			
Times tax rate 1)		40%	
Income tax payable/Current Tax Expense		a)	

Per discussion with client, the lawsuit will not be settled in 2015. RP

1) The company's effective tax rate is 40% (35% federal and 5% state)   RP

T = Traced payment to the cash disbursements journal

Note to student: You need to make two separate AJEs:

1)Record opening balance of deferred tax asset and liability

2)Record income tax expense and payable for 2014 and the 2014 change in deferred tax asset and liability. Do this adjustment on F-4.

Proli Footwear
Deferred Tax Analysis
December 31, 2014

	Balance per Client	Balance per Audit	Adjustment Required
Deferred Tax Asset	0		
Deferred Tax Liability	0		

	Future (Deductible)/ Taxable	Tax Rate	Deferred Tax Asset	Liability
Temporary Difference:				
Intangibles Amortization		40%		
Warranty liability		40%		
US Government vs. Proli		40%		
Estabon vs. Proli		40%		
Plant fire liability		40%		
Moccasins for All bankruptcy		40%		
Sales tax audit		40%		
Manufacturing overhead tax audit		40%		
Total Temporary Differences				
Deferred Tax Balances at 12/31/2014 Σa) = c)				
Deferred Tax Balances at 12/31/2013 Σb) = d)				
Change in deferred tax accounts c) - d)				

Notes from RP

--Bad debt expense for 2014 is the same as actual writeoffs.

--The writeoff of ostrich leather is deemed to meet IRS rules for the obsolete inventory deduction.

--Depreciation is the same for book and tax.

--Disregard meals and entertainment as an adjustment to taxable income.

--The client has never booked any deferred taxes, so the 12/31/13 balance needs to be calculated and recorded and then the 2014 change can be recorded. The only temporary differences at 12/31/2013 were intangibles amortization and warranty liability.

Temporary Differences at 12/31/2013:	Asset	Liability
Intangibles amortization-future taxable		
Warranty liability- future deductible		
Tax rate		
Deferred tax balances at 12/31/2013		

Note to student: You need to make two separate AJEs:

1) Record opening balance of deferred tax asset and liability

2)   Record income tax expense and payable for 2014 and the 2014 change in deferred tax asset and liability. Do this adjustment on F-4.

Proli Footwear
Temporary Differences Analysis – Intangible Assets
December 31, 2014

	Tax Amortization Period		Purchase Date	Cost	Impairment Loss per Auditors 2014	Expense per tax return 2014	Future (Deductible)/ Taxable 2014
Trademark Amortization Information							
Dapper™	SL 15 years	DB-2	2010	2,252,700			
Leatherworker™	SL 15 years	DB-2	1945	3,000			
Litetech™	SL 15 years	DB-2	1980	5,000			
Mudhoppers™	SL 15 years	DB-2	2012	2,641,800			
Proli™	SL 15 years	DB-2	1941	2,500			
Sportech™	SL 15 years	DB-2	2001	2,795,800			
Woodland™	SL 15 years	DB-2	2013	2,429,000			
Patent Amortization Information							
Patent #2698	SL 15 years	DB-3	1950	381,280			
Patent #6974	SL 15 years	DB-3	1999	609,500			
Patent #9767	SL 15 years	DB-3	2010	337,620			
Goodwill Amortization Information							
Purchase of Dapper Manufacturing Co.	SL 15 years	DB-4	2001	2,438,000			
Purchase of Softshoe, Inc.	SL 15 years	DB-4	2012	3,728,000			
Purchase of Woodland	SL 15 years	DB-4	2013	2,101,700			
Totals							

f

Note: Per IRS Publication 535, acquired patents, acquired trademarks and goodwill are Section 179 intangibles and must be amortized over 180 months (15 years). RP

184

©Proctor and Poli

Proli Footwear
Temporary Differences Analysis – Intangible Assets
December 31, 2013

	Tax Amortization Period		Purchase Date	Cost	Amortization Expense per Books 2013	Expense per tax return 2013	Future (Deductible)/ Taxable 2013
Trademark Amortization Information							
Dapper™	SL 15 years	DB-2	2010	2,252,700	56,318		
Leatherworker™	SL 15 years	DB-2	1945	3,000	0		
Litetech™	SL 15 years	DB-2	1980	5,000	125		
Mudhoppers™	SL 15 years	DB-2	2012	2,641,800	66,045		
Proli™	SL 15 years	DB-2	1941	2,500	0		
Sportech™	SL 15 years	DB-2	2001	2,795,800	69,895		
Woodland™	SL 15 years	DB-2	2013	2,429,000	60,725		
Patent Amortization Information							
Patent #2698	SL 15 years	DB-3	1950	381,280	0		
Patent #6974	SL 15 years	DB-3	1999	609,500	30,475		
Patent #9767	SL 15 years	DB-3	2010	337,620	16,881		
Goodwill Amortization Information							
Purchase of Dapper Manufacturing Co.	SL 15 years	DB-4	2001	2,438,000	60,950		
Purchase of Softshoe, Inc.	SL 15 years	DB-4	2012	3,728,000	745,600		
Purchase of Woodland	SL 15 years	DB-4	2013	2,101,700	52,543		
Totals					1,159,557		

f

185

©Proctor and Poli

Thumpem, Lumpem & Howe
ATTORNEYS AT LAW
Stamford, CT 06906

February 26, 2015

West & Fair CPAs, LLC
Stamford, CT

Gentlemen:

We have been requested by Proli Footwear, Inc. ("the Company"), to furnish you with certain information with reference to you examination of the Company's financial statements as of December 31, 2014.

1. The term "material" is defined as "greater than $50,000."

2. We are only aware of the following matters involving material pending or threatened litigation, claims, or assessments.

a. <u>U.S. Government vs. Proli</u>
    The U.S. Government and Proli are involved in a lawsuit concerning the dumping of toxic waste into the Housatonic River. The Government is assessing remediation costs of approximately $1,300,000. It is probable that the Government's claim in the amount of $600,000-$700,000 will prevail.

b. <u>Michael Estabon vs. Proli</u>
    Mr. Estabon is asserting that he suffered severe injuries from a fall which resulted from a defective heel in the Company's product. He is unable to work and is asserting economic damages in the amount of $850,000.   It is reasonably possible that this claim will prevail.

3. We are not aware of any material unasserted claims and/or assessments.

4. We understand that the Company represented or will be representing to you that there are no unasserted claims that we have advised it are probable of assertion and must be disclosed in accordance with Statement of Financial Accounting Standards No. 5. We agree with this representation.

5. We are informed that the Company understands that whenever, in the course of performing legal services for it with respect to a matter recognized to involve an unasserted possible claim or assessment that may call for financial statement disclosure, we have formed a professional conclusion that the Company should disclose or consider disclosure concerning such possible claim or assessment, as a matter of professional responsibility to the Company, we will so advise the Company and will consult with the Company concerning the question of such disclosure and the applicable requirements of Statement of Financial Accounting Standards No. 5. We hereby confirm that such understanding is correct.

6. Please be advised that our response is directed only to matters that have been given substantive attention by us in the form of legal consultation and, where appropriate, legal representations since March 1, 1998. In this connection, we have endeavored to determine from lawyers in our firm who have performed services for the Company whether such services involved advice concerning any litigation, controversies or claims of the type described above, but beyond that, we have made no independent review of any of the Company's transaction or contractual arrangement for purposes of this response.

7. The Company owed our firm $130,000 as of December 31, 2014.

This response includes matters that existed as of December 31, 2014, and during the period from that date to the date of this response.

Yours very truly,
Thumpem, Lumpem & Howe

Phillip Thumpem

By: Phillip Thumpem

Re: Proli Footwear – Fire at Walton, Florida Plant

On 1/30/15 I was contacted by John B. Fuddled, plant manager at the Walton facility. He stated that a fire had taken place on 1/29/15. Apparently a disgruntled employee, Victor Vishshoss, had intentionally started the fire and was apprehended after the damage was done. The fire destroyed part of the warehouse and the north end of the plant manufacturing facility. Criminal charges have been filed against Mr. Vishshoss.

The total loss is estimated to be about $1,800,000. Proli has a 10 percent deductible under its insurance policy with State FrameU Insurance. Therefore, $1,620, 000 will be covered by insurance. Controller Brian Baddude has indicated that the loss will be recorded in January 2015 with the following entry:

> Debit Loss on Plant Fire...................$180,000
> Credit Company Share of Fire Loss $180,000

Per Controller Brian Baddude, it is expected that this fire will result in a 10% reduction in production during the first quarter. It is the Company's intention to quickly make the repairs. There was no inventory stored where the fire occurred and no smoke damage occurred for any of the inventory. It is expected that this fire will have no effect on 2015 sales.

A determination must be made regarding what actions, if any, are required for the 2014 financial statements. I will discuss my findings with the audit team and Audit Manager.

1. Is any type of disclosure necessary in 2014? YES/NO

    a. Is footnote disclosure necessary? YES/NO Explain

    b. Is an audit adjustment required? YES/NO Explain

Re: Proli Footwear – Accounts Receivable from Moccasins for All

As a result of my discussions with Controller Brian Baddude, I was made aware that the accounts receivable from "Moccasins For All" in the amount of $550,068 has become uncollectible. On February 7, 2015, "Moccasins for All" filed chapter 7 bankruptcy in the federal district court in Bridgeport, CT.   Proli management does not expect to collect any of this receivable Controller Brian Baddude explained that his analysis of the Allowance for Bad Debts account required an additional accrual to cover this loss. He will make the adjustment in the February 2015.

Upon further review of the facts, I concluded that the financial condition of Moccasins had been deteriorating during 2014 and that they had slowed their payments to vendors during the fourth quarter of 2014.   However, the Proli credit department was unaware of the change in financial condition for Moccasins. Proli does not obtain updated credit reports for its customers on a regular basis. The last credit report for Moccasins was obtained in 2013.

A determination must be made regarding what actions, if any, are required for the 2014 financial statements. I will discuss my findings with the audit team and Audit Manager.

1. Is any type of disclosure necessary in 2014? YES/NO
    a. Is footnote disclosure necessary? YES/NO   Explain

    b. Is an audit adjustment required? YES/NO Explain

Re: Proli Footwear – Legal Invoice Review and Discovery of Undisclosed Legal Action

As a result of my review of legal and consulting invoices paid during the year, it came to my attention that there were invoices paid to the tax consulting firm of Dewey, Seamtobe, Truble & Ornot (DSTO) concerning tax audits initiated by the State of Connecticut Department of Revenue Security in October 2014.   A legal representation confirmation request was not sent to DSTO because Proli did not disclose this firm to us. Controller Brian Baddude explained that DSTO is not a law firm; it is a consulting firm based in Boston, MA that specializes in tax matters. Upon further investigation, it was determined that the State of Connecticut (SCT) is alleging two issues:

1. Proli failed to invoice and collect sales tax from certain customers for whom there was no resale certificate on file at Proli. Proli has countered that all their sales are to resellers and therefore no sales tax should be collected regardless of whether an executed tax waiver is on file. SCT is seeking unremitted sales taxes of $227,000 plus interest and penalties of another $62,000. Discussions are ongoing.
2. Proli incorrectly classified certain indirect manufacturing overhead costs as period expenses. SCT is alleging that Proli inappropriately reduced its income for the period ant that it owes approximately $122,000 including interest and penalties.

In my discussions with Controller Brian Baddude, he indicated that the actions by SCT were motivated by a budget shortfall crisis. Controller Brian Baddude further stated that the allegations did not have any basis in fact and that SCT is just looking for a soft touch! The conclusion of Richard Truble, partner at DSTO, was that the Sales Tax issue would be settled with zero tax liability for Proli. Richard Truble also concluded that the matter of the expense deduction issue would be settled for an amount less than $25,000.

Controller Baddude concluded that no entry or disclosure is necessary in the 2014 financial statements.

A determination must be made regarding what actions, if any, are required for the 2014 financial statements. I will discuss my findings with the audit team and Audit Manager.

1. ITEM 1 Questions: Is any type of disclosure necessary in 2014? YES/NO
   a. Is footnote disclosure necessary? YES/NO   Explain

   b. Is an audit adjustment required? YES/NO Explain
2. ITEM 2 Questions: Is any type of disclosure necessary in 2014? YES/NO
   a. Is footnote disclosure necessary? YES/NO   Explain

   b. Is an audit adjustment required? YES/NO Explain

Proli Footwear
AJE Control-Finishing the Audit
December 31, 2014

AJE Number	Reference	Accounts/Description	Account Number	Debit	Credit

x = account has impact on income before taxes amount

Impact on income before taxes =   DR/CR

Proli Footwear
Red Flag Events-Finishing the Audit
December 31, 2014

Event Number	Reference	Auditor Observation

Proli Footwear
Management Letter Comments-Finishing the Audit
December 31, 2014

Comment Number	Reference	Auditor Observation/ Recommendation	Benefit to Client

Proli Footwear
Time Control
December 31, 2014

Section	Budgeted Time	Time Spent Working with Team	Time Spent Working Alone
8. Finishing the Audit	4 hours		

Team member names:

ASSIGNMENT #9 – DRAFTING THE REPORT

ASSIGNMENT:

1. Complete each step of the drafting the report audit program. Indicate completion for each step by making sure that the step is initialed, dated, and that the workpaper reference is indicated. For those audit program steps that are already initialed as having been completed, enter an appropriate date and workpaper reference next to the initials.

AUDIT PROGRAM – DRAFTING THE REPORT

Procedures	Initials	Date	W/P Ref
Completing the Audit			
1. Draft the appropriate audit opinion subject to one of the following scenarios. Each situation is independent of the other situations.			
a. Proli Footwear's management refuses to accrue the accounts receivable loss related to the bankruptcy of Moccasins For All.			
b. The bank is expected to withdraw its financing because the Company has projections that indicate continued decrease in earnings and reduced revenues.			
c. The bank is expected to withdraw its financing because the Company has violated certain loan covenants that the bank will not waive.			
d. The auditors want to emphasize, in their opinion, the facts related to the fire that occurred in January.			
e. Proli Footwear's management refuses to accrue the warranty expense adjustments proposed by West & Fair.			
2. Prepare the management letter.	RW		

AUDIT MEMO
West & Fair CPAs, LLC
Stamford, CT

Re: Proli Footwear Proposed Audit Opinion

The following is the standard audit opinion. We will reference the PCAOB Standards in this report because Proli intends to go public in the near future.

We have audited the accompanying balance sheet of Proli Footwear, Inc. as of December 31, 2014, and the related statement of income, stockholders' equity, and cash flows for the year ended December 31, 2014. These financial statements are the responsibility of the Company's management. Our responsibility is to express an opinion on these financial statements based on our audit.

We conducted our audit in accordance with the standards of the Public Company Accounting Oversight Board (United States). Those standards require that we plan and perform the audit to obtain reasonable assurance about whether the financial statements are free of material misstatement. An audit includes examining, on a test basis, evidence supporting the amounts and disclosures in the financial statements. An audit also includes assessing the accounting principles used and significant estimates made by management, as well as evaluating the overall financial statement presentation. We believe that our audit provides a reasonable basis for our opinion.

In our opinion, the financial statements referred to above present fairly, in all material respects, the financial position of Proli Footwear, Inc. as of December 31, 2014 and the results of its operations and its cash flows for the year ended December 31, 2014, in conformity with accounting principles generally accepted in the United States of America.

We have also audited, in accordance with the standards of the Public Company Accounting Oversight Board (United States), Proli Footwear, Inc.'s internal control over financial reporting as of December 31, 2014, based on criteria established in the Internal Control - Integrated Framework issued by the Committee of Sponsoring Organizations of the Treadway Commission, and our report dated January , 2015, expressed an unqualified opinion thereon.

Section	Budgeted Time	Time Spent Working with Team	Time Spent Working Alone
9. Drafting the Report	2 hours		

Team Member Names:

Made in the USA
Charleston, SC
18 July 2012